The manual of improvisation

Charna Halpern
Del Close

edited by Kim "Howard" Johnson

Meriwether Publishing Ltd.
Colorado Springs, Colorado

Meriwether Publishing Ltd., Publisher
PO Box 7710
Colorado Springs, CO 80933-7710

Editor: Arthur L. Zapel
Cover design: Tom Myers

© Copyright MCMXCIV, MMI Charna Halpern, Del Close, Kim Johnson and Meriwether Publishing Ltd.
Printed in the United States of America
First Edition

All rights reserved. No part of this publication may be reproduced, stored in a retrieval system, or transmitted in any form or by any means, electronic, mechanical, photocopying, recording or otherwise, without permission of the publishers.

Library of Congress Cataloging-in-Publication Data

Halpern, Charna, 1952-
    Truth in Comedy : the manual for improvisation / by Charna Halpern, Del Close, and Kim "Howard" Johnson. -- 1st ed.
        p.   cm.
    ISBN 13: 978-156608-003-3
    ISBN 10: 1-56608-003-7
    1. Improvisation (Acting) 2. Stand-up comedy. I. Close, Del, 1934-1999.
II. Johnson, Kim, 1955- . III. Title.
PN2071.I5H26   1993
    792'.028--dc20
                                                   93-43701
                                                      CIP

       8   9   10   06   07   08

DEDICATIONS

Charna Halpern

*To my loving parents, Jack and Iris Halpern.
Without their constant calls to push me to continue
writing, this book might never have been finished.
I also thank them for raising me in a home that was
always filled with laughter.
... and to Rick Roman — wherever you are.*

Del Close

To Severn Darden, Elaine May and Theodore J. Flicker.

Kim "Howard" Johnson

*To Laurie Bradach, who improvises with me every day,
and for the Baron's Barracudas, who blazed the trail.*

ACKNOWLEDGMENTS

*So many have been so wonderful.
I'd like to send my thanks —*

To Bill Murray, Mike Myers, George Wendt, Chris Farley, Andy Richter, and Andy Dick for their support —

To Suzanne Plunkett, the best photographer in Chicago —

To Thom Bishop for his way with words —

To David Shepherd, Paul Sills, and Bill Williams for their inspiration —

To Betsy Nolan for being a perfectionist —

To "The Family" and all the other ImprovOlympic teams, for helping us to learn from them —

Special thanks to Kim Yale —

TABLE OF CONTENTS

Foreword by Mike Myers 1

Introduction I 3

Introduction II 6

CHAPTER ONE
What Is Improv, Anyway? 13

CHAPTER TWO
But Seriously, Folks... 23

CHAPTER THREE
Support and Trust 37

CHAPTER FOUR
Agreement 45

CHAPTER FIVE
Initiations and Game Moves 57

CHAPTER SIX
Moment to Moment to Moment 71

CHAPTER SEVEN
Building a Scene 81

CHAPTER EIGHT
One Mind, Many Bodies 91

CHAPTER NINE
Environmentally Aware 101

CHAPTER TEN
Responsibilities of a Harold Player 117

CHAPTER ELEVEN
How to Do a Harold 133

CHAPTER TWELVE
Harold As a Team Sport 149

About the Authors 151

FOREWORD

The end is in the beginning.

The Harold is an improv game that was introduced to me in Toronto, Canada, by Del Close and Charna Halpern. The first time I played the Harold it blew me away and it continues to blow me away to this day. The Harold isn't just a game — it's a way of looking at life. The basic principle of the Harold is adaptation, and being adaptive is the most crucial lesson I've learned. It provides you with a glossary of terms for the creative process and identifies recurring patterns in your imagination. It's the Zen approach to comedy. Most importantly, the Harold is a lot of fun.

Del Close, Charna Halpern and the Harold have been a major influence in my life. When I'm blocked I return to the methods of the Harold.

After all, the end is in the beginning.

— *Mike Myers*

INTRODUCTION I

I began producing the ImprovOlympic in 1981, after I met David Shepherd, one of the creators of Second City and the founder of the ImprovOlympic. David's inspiration came from ancient Greece, where the Olympian Games were a festival of sports, literature, music, and dance held every four years to honor Zeus, king of the gods. The Greeks saw the relationship between sports and the arts as innate. Both involved the exploration and extension of man's possibilities, rather than the perfection of his limitations (as is the case when art is reduced to arts and crafts and sports are reduced to stats and standings).

During our first year together, David and I developed separate visions for the ImprovOlympic, and we had a parting of the ways. I continued on to create an entertaining theatrical sport. In 1983, I found myself in need of inspiration. While the ImprovOlympic was a commercial success, it was beginning to look like a replica of Second City, which I wanted to avoid. Second City was already doing Second City quite well. I knew there was more to improvisation than three-minute scenes, but I wasn't sure what. I then met Del Close, who became a constant source of inspiration.

Del had a game to show me and my class, which he called "the Harold." This was not, however, the Harold we know and love today. Its nascent form was a little too large and chaotic for the stage. The trick would be preserving the chaos on stage while at the same time making it comprehensible. I showed Del one of my games called the Time Dash, a three-part scene where situations are carried out through spans of time.

We discovered that inserting the Time Dash along with my other short improvisational games into the Harold's long structure gave it a perfect form. Del and I felt like the people in the candy commercial who collide together. One says, "You've got chocolate in my peanut butter!" The other replies, "You've got peanut butter on my chocolate!" Hence, the birth of the Harold as it is known today.

Del and I have developed the newest advancement in improvisation. The Harold is now being done on college campuses all across the United States, as well as on the stages of the ImprovOlympic and Second City. In addition, the ImprovOlympic has become widely known as the best training ground for improvisers anywhere, a tradition Del started long ago with his training of John Belushi, Bill Murray, John Candy, Gilda Radner, and many others.

Our directors have been training top performance troupes to perform Harolds in our show, which has been referred to as the most daring game in town. Most importantly, we are continuing Del's tradition of fostering the finest talents of the future.

Those who have studied with us over the years have agreed that Del and I have discovered the "Truth" about successful improvisation. Because of our successful curriculum, I decided it was time to put it all down in a book so that others could be trained properly. When I suggested the idea to Del, he replied that it would be as much work as writing up a religion. He was less than excited about such a task. I can recall his words to this day: "You can do it, if you want."

As usual, Del was right. It was quite an undertaking. But after the book began taking shape, Del was there providing his usual expertise and divine inspiration.

I invite the reader to "come in" and discover our secrets. However, while the details of our instruction are here in this book, there is nothing as important as a good and clear director to solve the particular problems that can't always be foreseen in a book of this sort. The ImprovOlympic will provide those directors wherever they are needed.

In the past, people had labeled Del a "mad genius" because of his theories of improvisation. By now they've discovered he wasn't mad — he was *right*. Del has said that he is grateful that I have chosen to do his work his way. There is no mystery as to why I would choose to do this. His methods are correct, and his philosophies have provided us with the TRUTH IN COMEDY.

— *Charna Halpern*

INTRODUCTION II

The life of Del Close is virtually a history of American improvisation.

Del started his comedy career with Mike Nichols and Elaine May in the Compass Players in St. Louis during the 1950s.* Moving on to Second City and San Francisco's legendary Committee, Del returned to Second City in time to direct successes like John Belushi and Bill Murray. In fact, there are very few successful improvisers who have not worked with or been influenced by Del's work.

Although Del has worked on stage and screen throughout the years, he has been teaching or directing improv almost continuously since the 1950s and continues into the '90s.

Ed Asner, who began improvising in the '50s in the Playwright's Theatre Club at the University of Chicago, calls Del "a mad genius." Chris Farley, who joined *Saturday Night Live* after working with Del in the ImprovOlympic, says, "Del is the greatest teacher I've ever known. I would not be where I am today were it not for Del, that's for sure. I owe everything to Del. He brought me to Second City, and he taught me everything I needed to know."

Del's partner, Charna Halpern, was working with Compass Players founder David Shepherd in the early '80s in Chicago. When they went their separate ways, Charna joined forces with Del, and they began operating the ImprovOlympic. Their classes have turned out hundreds and hundreds of accomplished performers.

My own background in the early '80s included a fervent interest in comedy writing and performing; I had long been a fan of *Saturday Night Live* (where most of the performers had

---

*Actually, it could be argued that he began as a teenager, when he toured as a fire-eater with Dr. Dracula and his Tomb of Terrors; his duties included throwing handfuls of cooked spaghetti on the audience during a blackout when Dr. Dracula called for a plague of worms to descend upon them.

been directly influenced by Del) and Monty Python, becoming friends with the latter (working with them on *Life of Brian* and subsequently writing three books on the group).

I moved to Chicago and started studying at Second City. In those naive early days, I still thought improv and comedy were interchangeable terms. Del had by then departed Second City and started working with Charna and the ImprovOlympic, and word around Second City had it that Del was *the* person with whom to study improv. I immediately signed up for classes.

During the first year I spent studying with Del and Charna, Del would make occasional references to something called "the Harold." At the time, though, he was too busy trying to teach us the principles of simple scenes and games to elaborate.

Eventually, the details came. "Harold" was the name of a form of improv that Del had developed in the late 1960s while working with San Francisco's legendary improv troupe The Committee. The group was searching for some way to unite all their games, scenes, and techniques into one format; they developed a way to intertwine scenes, games, monologs, songs, and all manner of performance techniques.

They came up with one of the most sophisticated, rewarding forms of pure improv ever developed.

And then they had to name it.

A few years earlier, in *A Hard Day's Night,* a reporter asks George Harrison what he called his haircut. "Arthur," he responds.

So when Del asked his group what this exciting new form of improv should be called, one of his actors, Bill Mathieu, answered "Harold."

It has always been a minor annoyance for Del that his life's work has been saddled with such an inane, silly title. But the name stuck.

Saturday Night Live's Tim Kazurinski, who learned to play the Harold from Del at Second City, says he didn't really understand the name for many years.

"For years, I thought is was 'Herald.' I thought is was, in British terms, *heraldic,* with trumpeters that came out and heralded the cherubim and the seraphim! I thought it was a pronouncement about the topic selected by the audience," says Kazurinski. "Years later, I found out that it was 'Harold,' some guy's name. I once got into a big fight with someone about it. I was going 'Oh, no, no, it's a *much* more important title than that. Boy, are you stupid! You thought it was *Harold*?! And I was wrong — it's a dumb name for something really rather wonderful."

As I continued my improv studies we did some experimental performances with a new form of improv called Slow Comedy. It was interesting and exciting, but it wasn't Harold.

It wasn't until the following spring that Del and Charna had trained our groups thoroughly enough to revive the Harold before Chicago audiences. We ended up pitting teams against each other, letting the audiences vote for the winner. Harold became a unique sporting event and a theatrical competition.

The Harold was off and running, and it hasn't slowed down yet.

* * *

When I first heard that Charna wanted to do a book on the Harold, I was skeptical. Not because she doesn't have the credentials, but because I felt improv — and the Harold in particular — is a live experience, a living, breathing creature that can't fully be captured on paper.

But then I started thinking about all the potential improvisers scattered across the country that don't have easy access to Charna and Del. There are all sorts of eager comedy groups that will never advance beyond lame TV-show parodies without some sort of instruction. This is the guidebook they've been waiting for, the mother of all improv books, with Charna and Del telling what they know about Harold — which should be enough to keep most performers busy for the next few decades.

Harold is useful for more than performing, though. Harold training is beneficial for all sorts of people, from salespeople to public speakers. From personal experience, I know how improv is useful to writers: improvisers are trained to start their scenes in the middle and always eliminate clutter, principles that all good writers should implement.

One of the biggest misconceptions about improvisation is that only trained actors and comics can be successful. Actually, anyone can improvise. We all do it every day — none of us goes through our day to day life with a script to tell us what to do.

The simple, basic rules laid down in this book will result in much funnier, intelligent, and more interesting scenes. Deliberately trying to be funny or witty is a considerable drawback, and often leads to disaster. Honest responses are simpler and more effective. By the same token, making patterns and connections is much more important than making jokes.

This book should be looked on as a starting point; these are the blueprints that lay the groundwork. Real improv involves constant experimentation and exploration. Anyone who uses this book correctly will eventually make all sorts of original discoveries on his own — and that's part of the magic of the Harold.

Whether you're an experienced improviser or a curious neophyte, you're in for a treat. The Harold is the most exciting, innovative, funniest advanced form of improv yet devised — even if Del isn't fond of the name.

— Kim "Howard" Johnson

*If we want to see where we went wrong
We needn't look too far,
For where we'll be and where we've been
Is always where we are.
And everything that comes your way
Is something you once gave,
Somebody feels the water
Every time you make a wave.*

— Thom Bishop

CHAPTER ONE
What Is Improv, Anyway?

The word "improv" has been thrown around with reckless abandon over the years.

There is a national chain of comedy clubs called "The Improv," along with a TV series entitled *A Night at the Improv*.

Second City, where improvisation was refined and turned into a commercial success, continues to present comedy revues at its Chicago and Toronto locations, with touring companies traveling extensively.

And there are plenty of other performers doing improv comedy in clubs and theaters across the country.

The Improv clubs feature stand-up comics performing material that has been written, rehearsed, and polished in front of hundreds of audiences. They may throw in an authentic ad-lib or two during a performance, but very few of their acts are based on improvisation.

Second City today uses improvisation to develop material for their comedy revues. Many of their sketches are written, and then revised and perfected by improvising in front of an audience. Even the improv sets, performed nightly after the regular revues, rely heavily on material that is being developed for upcoming shows.

Then what exactly *is* improv?

Real improvisation is more than just a garnish, thrown like parsley onto a previously prepared stand-up comedy routine. Nor is it just a tool used to manufacture prepared scenes.

True improvisation is getting on-stage and performing without any preparation or planning.

Sounds easy, doesn't it? Even audience suggestions aren't

necessary. Strictly speaking, improvisation is making it up as you go along.

This definition makes all of us expert improvisers. We all go through life every day without a script, responding to our environment, making it up as we go along. Improvising on-stage is obviously a little different — the performers are trying to create while entertaining an audience.

Sure, improvisation was created to develop comedy for its own sake. Every writer or performer improvises as he or she creates, even if the only available audience is his typewriter or television set. Improvisation can be more than just a creative tool, though — it can be a vastly satisfying form of entertainment.

People often ask, "What do you use improvisation for? Is it to help an actor understand a role? To develop comedy material? As therapy?"

Improvisation is not some poor relation to "legitimate" theater, such as ballet or opera. It is an art form that stands on its own, with its own discipline and aesthetics. The roots of improv can be seen in the venerable and influential 16th-century theatrical form known as *commedia dell'arte*.

Improvisation can be seen as the 20th-century descendant of the *commedia*, with Harold as its most ebullient incarnation. Thus far, it hasn't gotten the respect it deserves from the "legitimate" theater community, but when it's properly considered a public art form, the question "What is it used for?" no longer applies.

This book is geared largely toward improvisation, and its role in discovering the truths about comedy. As the purists will be quick to point out, improvisation is not necessarily funny (even when it's intentional, as plenty of actors who have "died" on-stage will attest to). The first improvisations performed by the Compass Players and other forerunners to Second City were not always intended to be humorous.

In recent years, though, improv has become synonymous

with comedy. This slightly skewed image has come about through such aforementioned establishments as Second City, the Improv, and many others. Since this volume is geared toward truth in *comedy*, however, we will politely tip our hats in acknowledgment of the more serious uses of improvisation, and saunter off in the direction of chuckles, chortles, and guffaws.

HOW TO BE FUNNY

First of all, no one can read a book and become funny.

So, if you've just bought this book in the hopes of becoming popular, earning a reputation as a silver-tongued raconteur, or scoring points with the opposite sex, you might as well return this to the bookstore and exchange it for a copy of *1001 Jokes, Jests, and Jibes*.

That said, it *is* possible to learn techniques that teach you how to become a funny performer, and they don't involve memorizing pages of stale jokes. Everyone who has ever performed comedy has their own definite ideas about how to be funny. But the simplest and most basic concept may also be the most effective.

The truth is funny.

Honest discovery, observation, and reaction is better than contrived invention.

After all, we're funniest when we're just being ourselves. Sitting around relaxing with friends usually inspires far more laughter than a TV sitcom or someone trying to tell jokes. When was the last time you laughed out loud? Odds are that most of your recent belly laughs were the results of talking with friends.

When we're relaxing, we don't have to entertain each other with jokes. And when we're simply opening ourselves up to each other and being honest, we're usually funniest. We've all sat down with two or three friends and described an incident or discussed something that happened in our lives. This is

Truth in Comedy

precisely what a stand-up comic does, although a stand-up's audience is usually (though not always) larger than two or three people.

The freshest, most interesting comedy is not based on mother-in-law jokes or Jack Nicholson impressions, but on exposing our own personalities. One of the most disquieting moments for a novice performer is when he (or she) gets a laugh that is completely unexpected. Improvisers often like to feel "in control" of scenes; such laughter tends to prove just the opposite is occurring.

Giving up control may be disastrous for a stand-up comic, but an improviser has to put his trust into the hands of the ensemble, and be prepared for those inevitable, frightening mystery laughs — no matter how embarrassing they may be. As Steve Martin says, "Comedy is not pretty." Just let it happen.

When an improviser lets go and trusts his fellow performers, it's a wonderful, liberating experience that stems from group support.

A truly funny scene is not the result of someone trying to steal laughs at the expense of his partner, but of generosity — of trying to make the other person (and his ideas) look as good as possible.

Real humor does not come from sacrificing the reality of a moment in order to crack a cheap joke, but in finding the joke in the reality of the moment.

Simply put, in comedy, honesty is the best policy.

HAPPILY EVER AFTER

Following the rules of a game and remaining true to a premise generally results in much bigger laughs than inventing witty statements.

When Del was directing a Second City company in Toronto that included Dan Ackroyd, Dave Thomas, and Gilda Radner, they began playing an improv game called "Happily

Ever After." The premise is a simple one: an improv group presents a popular fairy tale, beginning with the moment the tale traditionally ends ("They lived happily ever after.").

This company picked "Hansel and Gretel," beginning just after the children push the Wicked Witch into the oven. A simple premise to go on. The performers were wise enough to use the characters and situations that were established in the original fairy tale, rather than invent new ones in hopes of laughs. They were savvy enough to trust that there was enough material in the real "Hansel and Gretel" to make their follow-up highly entertaining — and they were right.

As the narrator, Dan Ackroyd picked up on the rather grisly ending of the story and merely extrapolated from the situation. The story presented by the company began with people — including a number of woodcutters — disappearing from the Black Forest, never to be heard from again. A search party eventually discovered two cannibal children — Hansel and Gretel (Dave Thomas and Gilda Radner) — in the woods. As explained by Ackroyd, after the children had pushed the Witch in the oven, they ate her. Subsequently, they acquired a taste for human flesh, and the two young cannibals began preying on victims in the woods. The children were then put on trial in Germany during World War II, and the company staged a parody of the Nuremberg War Trials.

Even though the scene took some very peculiar twists, it was all rooted in the premise put forth in the original fairy tale, instead of inventing situations and lines for cheap jokes. Ackroyd simply hypothesized — from the original ending of pushing the Witch in the oven — that the children then decided to taste her. Everything else in the scene stems directly from there!

HAROLD WHO?

If honesty is the best road to comedic improvisation, the best vehicle to get us there is Harold.

Simply put, it is the ultimate in improvisation.

The Harold is like the space shuttle, incorporating all of the developments and discoveries that have gone before it into one new, superior design.

All of the discoveries made about creating scenes, all of the games that have been developed, all of the principles regarding truth in comedy, can become part of the cohesive, unified whole that is the Harold.

Skilled Harold players take all of these disparate ingredients and build something much greater than the sum of its parts.

Uninitiated audiences watching a Harold for the first time seldom know what to expect. What they see is a full company of improvisers on stage who do nothing *but* improvise from start to finish, something quite rare in the world of comedy.

==The first rule in Harold is that there are no rules. Still, a basic Harold usually takes on a general structure described as follows.==

Harold begins with a group of players — six or seven is usually ideal (although successful Harolds have been performed with fewer than five persons and as many as 10 or 12). When the group steps onto the stage, they may want to check out the performing space, looking for aspects of it that can be incorporated into the Harold. The team solicits a suggestion for a theme from the audience, and begins a warm-up game to share their ideas and attitudes about the theme. The warm-up can be very physical, or it can be as simple as a game of word association.

Eventually, a couple of players usually start a scene. Normally, it's unrelated to the theme, although it can be inspired by elements of the warm-up game. Once the scene is established, it will be cut off by a second scene, one which has as little to do with the first scene as it has to do with the theme. After a third scene is similarly presented, the ensemble will then participate in what is generally referred to as a "game," although the event may bear little resemblance to the audience's notion of a game.

The initial three scenes usually return again. This time, they may have some bearing on the theme. Or, maybe not. After a second group game, the scenes return for one last time, often tying into each other and the theme, culminating in a finale that incorporates the theme and as many elements from the scenes and games as possible.

It may sound complicated to the uninitiated, but its structure is similar to a three-act play. When it's performed by a group of trained improvisers, the results can be spectacular.

To put it another way, a Harold is a lot like sex. When it is good, it's very good. When it is bad, it's still pretty good.

Del tells about seeing Jim Belushi run off stage after a particularly inspired improvisation, shouting, "This is better than sex!" In fact, anyone who has participated in a really good Harold knows the indescribable rush that accompanies it.

Earlier Harolds were not as refined as they became during the ImprovOlympia, though they were still very useful, says Tim Kazurinski, who studied with Del at Second City in the late 1970s.

"When we did the Harold back then, we'd take an audience suggestion and line up against the back wall. Alternately, we would begin coming forward in groups of two, starting scenes that really weren't going anywhere yet. Another couple would cut you off or you would fade to the back wall when you were tiring. You would keep this up for 15 or 20 minutes, until all these little vignettes began to tie up or interweave," explains Kazurinski.

"What seemed like a dopey little scenario early in the piece now started to take shape, as other people started joining that scene, and it became a recurring scene or 'runner.' When it was really humming, they would all mesh, and make a statement that was more of a tableau. Everything that you had done up to that point was synthesized in that final scene or conglomeration of scenes. What had washed over the audience was a really fascinating 20- or 30-scene barrage about this topic, more than you ever knew — or possibly wanted to know — about the selected topic.

"When it works, it's an amazing thing. And when it doesn't, the audience thinks you're insane," he laughs. "But something good always comes from it. Even if we missed the mark, there were usually enough interesting events happening to make people think about that topic."

Saturday Night Live's Chris Farley, an ImprovOlympic alumnus, loves the unpredictability of the Harold.

"Anything can happen," says Farley. "It is something that is created slowly, out of the moment. It's spontaneous and magic."

Another of Del's illustrious alumni is George Wendt of *Cheers* fame, who Del directed at Second City. Wendt agrees the Harold is terrific, both for performance and for developing new comedic material.

"We never did quite enough Harolds at Second City," remarks Wendt. "I always felt that when done correctly, the Harold is the most magical, wonderful improvisational experience you can have, both for the audience and for the company. Very satisfying. But even if it wasn't entirely clicking as a performance piece, it was invaluable. I thought it was the best way to create material.

"To me, taking a theme and working on your feet — without discussions, qualifications, setups, blackouts, and the like — is a much purer and easier way to find kernels of scenes that could be expanded and written," explains Wendt.

"The exact opposite would be the Second City approach, which is to take a bunch of suggestions and write them on a piece of paper, stand backstage in the Green Room, and stare at a blackboard with a bunch of suggestions on it — basically stare at words. I got nothing from that. Second City was a constant struggle for me in terms of it being fun to improvise, and in terms of creating material."

In contrast, he describes the Harold as a completely emancipating experience.

"Harold is like jumping out of an airplane! It's like being thrown into the water — you've got to sink or swim," exclaims Wendt. "The very intensity of the pressure to create is liberating."

According to Wendt, a good Harold is not only fun for the performers and their audience, it's also a great way to come up with ideas for future material.

"It's a wonderful thing in and of itself, and as a means to an end — creating material — it's equally wonderful. If you do a half-hour Harold, and you don't come out of that thing with at least a blackout, you've had a pretty lame night," says Wendt. "Conversely, if you do a half-hour Harold and you come out of it with a killer blackout, it's been well worth it!"

Like so many successful performers, George Wendt values his Harold training. These skills, which have proven so useful to others, are presented in these pages. This book is designed to provide training which, when practiced with like-minded souls, will let you "see Harold."

KEY POINTS FOR CHAPTER ONE

*Be honest.

*Don't go for the jokes.

*There's nothing funnier than the truth.

CHAPTER TWO
But Seriously, Folks . . .

One of the biggest mistakes an improviser can make is attempting to be funny.

In fact, if an audience senses that any performer is deliberately trying to be funny, that performer may have made his task more difficult (this isn't always the case for an established comedian playing before a sympathetic crowd — comics like Jack Benny and Red Skelton were notorious for breaking up during their sketches, and their audiences didn't seem to mind it a bit. A novice performer isn't usually as lucky, unless he's managed to win the crowd over to his side).

When an actor gives the unspoken message "Watch this, folks, it's really going to be funny," the audience often reads this as "This is going to be so funny, I'm going to make you laugh whether you want to or not." Human nature being what it is, many audience members respond to this challenge with "Oh, yeah? Just go ahead and try, because I'm not laughing," to the performer's horror.

A much easier approach for improvisers is to be sincere and honest, drawing the audience into the scene rather than reaching out and trying to pull them along.

Improvisers can be relaxed and natural, knowing that if they are sincere, the audience will be more receptive to them. Audience members laugh at things they can relate to, but they cannot empathize if the performers are insincere.

Ars est celare artem, as the ancient Romans would say: the art is in concealing the art.

COMEDY AND KUNG FU

In a recent class, Del discussed the importance of taking improv seriously, and not letting the audience affect the integrity of the work. Speaking in the performance space — a theatre above a bar that features bands in between improv shows — he compared it to the work of martial artists:

"I feel a little silly at times, saying how seriously this work must be taken. Look around us. There's lots of goofy shit all over the walls, we know what's served on the tables, and we share the space with blues bands of varying degrees and quality. And we have an audience that will be satisfied with much less than we're capable of giving them. It is not that the environment is particularly supportive to group-experimental-improvisation performance art — it's more like the comedy saloon!

"When you walk into a dojo, there is a change that comes over you. The environment is supportive of the concept — which is to study martial arts. You've seen them when you walk down the street; people in there grabbing each other's pajamas and throwing each other to the floor.

"There are a few squares in our society that think kung fu is about kicking people's heads in, but we know differently. It is something else. It is a martial *art*. You don't walk into a dojo and say 'Good morning, master, I'd like to learn how to kick somebody's head in, please.' They'd throw you down the stairs! It would be like going to Jesus and saying 'I'd like to learn how to walk on water, please.' I mean, there are more important things to do!

"Coming here to learn to make people laugh is equally absurd. To assume that making the audience laugh is the goal of improvisation is almost as absurd as assuming that you go to a dojo to learn how to kick somebody's face in. It's just not true!

"Still, they laugh. It is a side-effect of attempting to achieve something more beautiful, honest, and truthful, something that has far more to do with the theatre — which puts your attention on what is important about being a human in a community — as opposed to television entertainment, which is designed to take your mind *off* what is more important about your lives.

"It is easy to become deluded by the audience, because they laugh. Don't let them make you buy the lie that what you're doing is for the laughter. Is what we're doing comedy? Probably not. Is it funny? Probably yes. Where do the really best laughs come from? Terrific connections made intellectually, or terrific revelations made emotionally."

NO LAUGHING ALOUD

Physicist Niels Bohr once said, "Some things are so serious, they can only be joked about."

Likewise, the only way to do a comedy scene is to play it completely straight.

The more ridiculous the situation, the more seriously it must be played; the actors must be totally committed to their characters and play them with complete integrity to achieve maximum laughs.

Airplane! and the two *Naked Gun* movies are perfect examples. The three films' lines, situations, and sight gags are so outrageous that they must have a solid anchor. Therefore, the Zucker brothers hired an established dramatic actor, Leslie Nielsen, to deliver the silliest lines completely deadpan. In *The Naked Gun,* his performance as Lt. Frank Drebbin is almost identical to his performances in the various TV police dramas that are being lampooned. Any twinkle in his eye or winking at the camera to let audiences know that he is in on the laugh would destroy the credibility and integrity he has built up, which make the jokes so effective.

One beginning ImprovOlympic student announced to co-author Halpern that he was studying improvisation, but then planned to go on to "serious" acting. "What do you think you're supposed to be doing now?" she asked him.

Famed commercial director Joe Sedelmeier once said that when he auditions comic actors, he immediately dismisses anyone who asks whether the script should be read seriously or humorously. He knows that if they have to ask, they obviously don't know what they're doing. ==The only way to play comedy is seriously.==

A JOKE AND A LAUGH

The most direct path to disaster in improvisation is trying to make jokes. This is so important, it deserves repeating.

==*Don't try to make jokes in improv!*==

Jokes are not necessary; they are a complete waste of time and energy that is better spent developing a scene. Get the point? Chances are if you're concentrating on telling a joke, you're not looking for the connections in a scene. And the connections will draw much bigger laughs than any joke.

Many actors don't understand the difference between a joke and a laugh. A joke is only one way — and seldom the best way — to get a laugh; jokes can get laughs but, obviously, laughs don't always result from jokes.

The most effective, satisfying laughs usually come from an actor making a connection to something that has gone before. The connecting line must be truly inspired by the situation on the stage at the moment, and usually can't be planned or recreated later. It is seldom the least bit funny out of context. A laugh resulting from a connection is a classic example of a moment when "you had to be there," and describing what happened later can't do it justice.

Standing on stage and telling the audience a joke in the middle of a scene sucks the energy out of a scene. Making a connection generates energy for that scene; as connections are discovered, they perpetuate themselves, raising the scene to a level which could never be reached by telling jokes.

JOKES

Jokes are more primitive, basic and direct — I tell you something I think is funny, hoping you will respond by laughing. A comedian who tells jokes is basically a salesman, trying to sell the audience a clever story or punch line, while hoping to be paid back in laughter. On a good night, he may sell his entire line, but on a bad night, he may suffer the equivalent of having every door slammed shut in his face.

A good improviser doesn't need to resort to jokes; jokes are born out of desperation, and the audience is the first to realize it. When players worry that a scene isn't funny, they may resort to jokes. This usually *guarantees* that the scene won't be funny.

When a player forces a joke, it is usually a comment about the scene. Unfortunately, if you are able to comment on the scene, then you are not really involved in the scene. Many of our great comedians will deliver a funny aside to the camera, although they are generally making a joke at the expense of emotional commitment. This may be fine for the joke-tellers, but when improvisers resort to such tactics, they quickly find that they don't have the faculties — or the writers — of a Jack Benny.

In so many of the classic Marx Brothers comedies, Groucho leans over to the camera and makes a funny comment about one of his brothers or Margaret Dumont. It works well within the context of the picture, but Groucho wasn't improvising. Besides, we all know how much emotional depth Groucho brought to his love scenes with Dumont. Likewise, on *The Burns and Allen Show,* George Burns is able to tune in a TV set to see what scheme Gracie is cooking up, making his remarks directly to the audience. Funny? Yes, but it's not improvisation. It's hard to be drawn into a scene when Burns can step out of that scene at any moment and make funny comments.

Funny asides to the audience have their place; commenting on a scene is even allowable in improv under certain circumstances, *but only as long as you aren't involved in the scene at the time* (unless it becomes a game in itself — a matter we'll discuss later). The situation is similar to a relationship between a man and a woman — the more they talk about it, the less time they spend on it.

Jokes frequently lead to groans from an audience — they rarely get laughs. On those occasions when they do get laughs, it is usually at the expense of the scene, because the level of commitment to the scene is lowered. Jokes tend to be employed as a last-ditch measure by insecure players when they are worried that a scene isn't funny. Unfortunately, too many players manage to establish themselves as bad improvisers and humorless stand-up comics in the same scene.

If a player begins making jokes at the expense of a scene, he has nothing to fall back on when the jokes fail. If a scene is not getting laughs, however, the performers don't need to worry, as long as they are being true to their scene. They only need to be patient. The laughs will come soon enough from connections — and the connections cannot be avoided.

CONNECTIONS

Audiences appreciate a sophisticated game player. When a player listens and uses patterns that have developed in a scene, it can elicit cheers from an audience which are much more intoxicating than the laughs that result from a few jokes.

Del Close remembers hearing famed comic Lenny Bruce talk on stage for 20 minutes without getting one laugh — and then suddenly tying together several trains of thought with one or two sentences, as the audience erupted in cheers at the brilliance they had just witnessed.

Those sorts of cheers are far more rewarding than a few laughs. When properly played, a Harold audience resembles the crowd at a sporting event rather than the audience at a nightclub. A Harold audience will react as if they've seen a Michael Jordan slam-dunk when they watch players remembering each other's ideas and incorporating them back into their scenes. We have witnessed standing ovations when a player pulls together eight different trains of thought in one brief monolog. Those cheers and screams can become even more addicting than laughs.

==Making connections is as easy as listening, remembering, and recyling information. When patterns in scenes are noticed== *and played* they create continuity in the scene.

A player must first listen to what his fellow players are saying, which he can't do if he's busy inventing jokes and trying to force the scene in one particular direction. He has to store the information in the back of his mind, not relying on it too heavily, but keeping it handy so he can pull it out when something in the scene triggers the connection. When such an opportunity arises in the scene, the player recycles the thought or action. The audience members make the connection for themselves, and respond much more enthusiastically than if they had just heard a punch line.

Connections are a much more sophisticated way to get laughs. When an audience sees the players start a pattern, they finish the connections in their own minds. They are forced to think just a tiny bit, and when they have to work along with the players to recognize the laugh, it is much more gratifying for the audience, which has had its intelligence flattered in the bargain.

The simplest, most basic example of connections can be seen in a pattern game.

THE PATTERN GAME: LEARNING TO MAKE CONNECTIONS

The Pattern Game is basically a word association game. The players take turns calling out words and short phrases inspired by previous words and phrases, in order to connect as many pieces of information as possible.

Truth in Comedy

Connections made during the game moves will allow players to discover different levels of meaning to their ideas, as well as inspire additional ideas for the scenes to come. The Pattern Game is a great way to demonstrate the principle of "Finding Order Out of Chaos."

Among other uses, the Pattern Game is the beginning of the process of engendering a "Group Mind," something that we'll delve into much deeper in the chapters to come. When the Pattern Game is used as the opening exercise for a Harold, the audience sees the group developing its point of view toward its theme; this happens as the group shares information, ideas, and attitudes.

Different groups operating on the same suggestion will usually come up with totally different sets of ideas; one group can play the Pattern Game twice with the same suggestion and probably end up with different results. The game is really a process of discovery and exploration to prepare a group for the main event.

THE PATTERN GAME: EXAMPLE 1

Here are two separate pattern games, done by different groups, but both based on the suggested theme "dog":

Team A

"Collar."

"Police."

"K-9."

"Rin Tin Tin."

"Barking up the wrong tree."

"Firemen."

"101 Dalmatians."

"Open 24 hours."

"I read it in the Sunday papers."

"Sentence."

"Death."

"Bergman."

"Bird dog."

"Bird Man of Alcatraz."

"Prison."

"Bondage."

"Collar."

Team B

"Loyalty."

"Man's best friend."

"Barking."

"Sit."

"You can have the kids. I'll take the dog."

"Stay."

"Caged."

"Divorce."

"Heel."

"Barking."

"Cat fight."

"His bark is worse than his bite."

"He's a stray."

Team A's use of the "dog" theme revealed ideas about crime and punishment; Team B discovered levels of failed human relationships, in addition to animal-human relationships.

PATTERN-MAKING MADE EASY

As shown in the previous examples, the Pattern Game requires players to heighten the moves, but not to comment or explain them to the audience. It has to be played thoughtfully, and each player's response should be based on the meaning of what has gone before, not on wit utilized for a cheap laugh. If a player responds with the word "sex," the next player should know better than to respond with "fun" or "not enough." These may be personal opinions, but a better and more intelligent response would be to phrase those opinions into a move that forwards the game. "Sex" may make a player think of "blue eyes," which leads someone else to respond with "Paul Newman," prompting a subsequent player to name his favorite Paul Newman movie. Combining the meanings of these moves eventually results in the formation of definite themes.

There are different methods of playing the Pattern Game and an experienced player will discover more sophisticated game moves. One of these is known as "skipping a joke." If one player says "Harry Truman" and the next player responds with "Breakfast at Tiffany's," a hip audience will appreciate the fact that they've skipped over the obvious, "Truman Capote." The more familiar a group becomes with the Pattern Game, the more variations and refinements they'll discover.

All of the themes developed during the course of the game become themes for the Harold, and the tiniest, most innocuous phrase used is fair game for use in the main body of the Harold itself.

Even though the suggestion from the audience provides the inspiration for the Harold, the theme itself is developed by the players during the Pattern Game. The teams raise the level of the audience suggestion as they explore what it means to each of them — no matter how banal the suggestion from the audience may seem, the players will make it profound.

THE PATTERN GAME: EXAMPLE TWO

Some Pattern Games circle back to the first move made, but others encompass the entire outline for the scenes in a Harold, such as the following game based on an audience suggestion of "Camera":

"High school."

"High speed."
"Dope."
"Indy 500."
"Most likely to . . ."
"Crash and burn."
"In memoriam."
"Viet Nam."
"Don't write on the wall."
"Smokin'."
"I caught you."
"Smile!"
"I think I got it."
"Clap."
"I think I got it."
"The answer is . . ."
"Let's see what develops."
"I think I got it."
"Photo finish."
"By a nose."
"Buy a vowel."
"By the hair of my chinny chin chin."
"Buying a bond."
"Propaganda."
"Buy it."
"Viet Nam."
"Bye, bye."
"Dope."
"Speed."
"It happened so fast."
"Indy 500."
"High speed."
"High school."

Truth in Comedy

This Pattern Game inspired scenes with numerous levels, following the lives of four youths through high school — a fast-paced life of fast cars, drugs, sex, and smokin' in the boys' room, progressing to their Viet Nam experiences. A scene about the Viet Nam memorial was inspired by connections to reading the bathroom wall in high school.

It all resulted from the simple method of ordering information through a unique method of communication — the Pattern Game.

THE RULES OF THE GAME

Throughout this book, we will be using examples of different improv games to underscore the comedic principles involved. There is some similarity to playing games like Hide-and-Seek, inasmuch as there are basic rules of each game that must be understood and followed.

Anyone can improvise, but like any game, if the players don't learn and obey the rules, no one will play with them. In childhood games like Cowboys and Indians or Cops and Robbers, if someone is shot, he has to "die." If he is taken prisoner and tied up, he has to remain tied up until someone frees him. A child who doesn't follow these rules won't be very popular in his neighborhood.

There are plenty of rules in improvisation, as a quick thumb through this book will show. However, one of the first rules is "There are no rules." Just about any rule here can be broken *under the proper circumstances;* the guidelines in the following chapters demonstrate when a rule can be broken as part of an appropriate game move.

During his years at Second City, George Wendt says that the "no rules" rule could be both liberating and frustrating while improvising for Del.

"Our working relationship was extremely loose," he recalls. "Almost anarchic, to the extent that Del would either ignore scenes or give copious notes on scenes that were eminently forgettable! It was alternately enlightening and discouraging, as it would be for any improv company. You'd do a brilliant scene and you'd know it was brilliant, and the audience would know it was brilliant, and everybody would be very excited. You'd come backstage and Del would say, 'Nice work in the psychiatrist scene. Unfortunately, Mike Nichols and Elaine May did it in 1963!' "

Anything can happen in improv. The only rule that can *never* be broken is the rule of agreement. Experienced improvisers may decide to cut loose in a scene and break as many improv rules as possible, and the scenes are usually very funny (at least to fellow improvisers — they run the risk of being a bit in-jokey to other observers). Even here, though, they are simply playing a game — the "Rule-Breaking Game," and the performers all agree to participate.

If the game rules of improvisation are followed, the players will "win" on stage. And if they play the game well, then everybody wins.

KEY POINTS FOR CHAPTER TWO

*Don't make jokes.

*Let humor arise out of the situation.

*Take the scene seriously.

*Agreement is the only rule that cannot be broken.

*Connections cannot be avoided; don't force them.

CHAPTER THREE
Support and Trust

The actor's business is to justify.
— Elaine May
St. Louis Compass Players, 1957

The master weaver incorporated the mistakes of his students into a larger pattern.
— Sufi saying

Many years ago, Del was teaching an improv class during the same period he was directing The Committee in San Francisco. In order to impress upon them the importance of trust among actors, he decided to employ an exercise often used in acting classes. "We had a second-level balcony in our theatre," he recalls. "As a display of trust, I leaped off the balcony into the arms of the students. They dropped me.

"In order to give them the impression that they were not failures, I climbed up again and jumped off a second time. They dropped me again. I found out shortly after that one of those falls had broken my collarbone!" he laughs.

Fortunately, most "trust exercises" end far more successfully. Broken bones aside, falling off a platform doesn't even come close to the fear an actor feels when he realizes he is not being supported in a scene by his fellow players. That chilling realization is more like jumping out of a plane and realizing your parachute is still on board.

Support and trust go hand-in-hand for performers; they must trust that their fellow players will support them. The only star in improv is the ensemble itself; if everyone is doing his job well, then no one should stand out. *The best way for an improviser to look good is by making his fellow players look good.*

When former Second City and ImprovOlympic actor David Pasquesi won a Chicago award for performing, he accepted it by saying, "Our job is to make the others look good. By getting this award, I guess I'm not doing my job. I'll try harder next time!"

If the ensemble members commit 100 per cent to the group, there will be no mistakes on stage.

"I don't see how any actor could not do that," says Chris Farley, emphasizing the importance of the actor committing to his scene. "What else could they do? That's what they're doing. They're on the stage for that purpose. Anything else is not giving 100 per cent, and if that's what you really want to do, then *give* 100 per cent."

Farley recalls that Michael Myers (his future *Saturday Night Live* co-star) was a performer in the very first Harold he ever saw, and was impressed at the way Myers and the others were so committed to the work that they were able to take chances during the show which they otherwise couldn't have.

"I remember watching Mike and being truly in awe of how everything evolved from a mere suggestion," remembers Farley. "Mike was able to use the audience quite a bit, going out into the audience and not being limited by the space on the stage, tackling any idea. Del talks about stepping off the cliff, and Mike is one that definitely steps off the cliff and takes a chance — takes many chances. He initiated and furthered the Harold to depths unknown — it was really amazing."

When performers truly commit to a scene, they take care of each other. Whenever someone makes what appears to be a mistake on stage, the others will immediately justify it and weave it into the pattern of the entire work. More often than not, those "mistakes" become valuable contributions to the piece. The entire ensemble winds up looking brilliant because, like the Sufi weaver, they acknowledge mistakes and incorporate them into the larger work to add extra texture and depth.

In other words, *justify!* If a scene fails because a player makes a wrong move, the whole group must share the blame if they didn't justify the move. Each improviser shares a small portion of responsibility for the piece on stage. They must focus their concentration on the work of the group — *not* the work of any individual.

One other approach, according to Del, is to attack the stage — advice which Chris Farley took to heart during his very first improv class with Del.

"I got up there and tried to impress him with as much sweat and blood as I knew how, because that's all I had," says Farley. "I just went up there with as much physical movement as I could, because that's all I knew. I could do physical movement because I played football. Maybe I was *too* aggressive because I was nervous.

"I remember reading that Del told John Belushi to attack the stage, and so I tried to attack the stage like Belushi. He said 'Settle down, son! You're sweating too hard. You're like the guys they strap to the front of a battleship when they go into battle — fearless, but you have to have some control, too.' That's one of the first things he ever said to me, and he taught me the balance. He taught me everything I know," says Farley.

"From Del, I learned to face my fear. He taught me to follow that fear and trust that something will come to me, to step off the cliff and take a risk."

Of course, it's much easier to fearlessly attack the stage when a player can trust his teammates to support him. One of the best ways to teach support and trust — and reinforce the use of patterns and connections — is through a game called "The Hot Spot."

THE HOT SPOT

When "The Hot Spot" is played correctly, it's a joy to behold, and even more enjoyable to create. When it's not done well, it can be excruciatingly embarrassing for all concerned.

This game utilizes several of the previously discussed improv principles. The Hot Spot demonstrates how easy it is to make connections, even when players don't realize they are doing so; it also teaches the absolute necessity of players supporting each other. Students quickly learn that the game is more important than its individual players; egos have to be sacrificed for the good of the game. The greater the trust, the faster and funnier the game.

The rules are actually quite simple. The players gather on stage in a loose half-circle around an imaginary "hot spot," located down stage center. The group must create a musical pattern of ideas, using lines from real songs, inspired by a previous scene or the general theme of the piece.

To do this, one person stands firmly on the hot spot. He has the "spotlight," and must begin a song, singing loudly and confidently.

Before he can finish the second line, however, another player literally pushes him off of the hot spot. The new player loudly and confidently begins singing a different song that has been inspired by the one he has just heard.

He is immediately interrupted by a third player, who knocks *him* off the hot spot and begins singing another song, similar in theme. This continues at a fast pace, with players bumping each other away at a rapid clip (just as acts used to get the "hook" in vaudeville days).

Each of the players is responsible for keeping the game moving at a very fast pace by pushing each other off the hot spot as soon as the idea has been conveyed. *Game moves may — and should be — repeated to keep the pattern circling back.*

EXAMPLE: If the theme of the Hot Spot was "Sex," the game might start out with players singing the following:

PLAYER ONE: "I'm just a girl who can't say no —"
PLAYER TWO: "But will you love me tomorrow —"
PLAYER THREE: "Girls just want to have fun —"

PLAYER FOUR: "When will you marry me, Bill —"

Obviously, this is the beginning of a pattern of songs dealing with commitment (or the lack of) in relationships. This might be inspired by the theme of sex.

Another example of the Hot Spot was used in a Harold inspired by the theme of "growing up." These songs actually built the story of a life, while returning to key points of that life:

PLAYER ONE: "Happy birthday to you —"

PLAYER TWO: "I won't grow up! I don't want to go to school —"

PLAYER THREE: "Smokin' in the boys' room —"

PLAYER FOUR: "When I was 17, it was a very good year —"

PLAYER ONE: "Happy birthday to you —"

PLAYER THREE: "When I was 21, it was a very good year —"

PLAYER TWO: "When Johnny comes marching home again, hurrah, hurrah —"

PLAYER FOUR: "Get a job, sha na na na —"

PLAYER FIVE: "Workin' nine to five, what a way to make a livin' —"

PLAYER TWO: "Take this job and shove it, I ain't workin' here no more —"

PLAYER ONE: "Happy birthday to you —"

PLAYER TWO: "When I was 35, it was a very good year —"

PLAYER FOUR: "When I get older, losing my hair, many years from now —"

PLAYER FIVE: "Old man, take a look at my life, I'm a lot like you —"

PLAYER TWO: "Day is done, gone the sun —"

Clearly, the players dealt with birth, childhood, school, the army, jobs, marriage, and death — a musical pattern

Truth in Comedy

exploring the idea of growing up in the Hot Spot!

As a theme emerges, the game takes on its own pace. The Hot Spot is similar to the Pattern Game, but the music and physical elements of the Hot Spot result in a wilder, more frenetic pace.

(This is also a good game for a large number of players, and is sometimes played with two or more teams; 10, 15, or even 20 players can create an effective, highly charged "Hot Spot" game.)

Even if the players don't have a song in mind, they should still be encouraged to push each other off the hot spot, for several reasons.

Primarily, this is a perfect opportunity for players to exhibit support for their fellow players. The best way to support the teammate on the hot spot is to rudely shove him off that spot.

The game is at stake here. If one player is stuck on the hot spot for too long, he grows embarrassed; even worse it makes the group look like it isn't working together. And if that player has to sing more than two lines, it isn't.

Again, the only way for the group to look good is for each of its members to commit himself to keeping the game moving rapidly. When a player jumps out without an idea, he discovers that a song sung off the top of his head at the spur of the moment usually connects to the theme better than anything devised while waiting on the sidelines.

The Hot Spot is a great opportunity for a player to put his mind to the test, to see how it kicks in during an emergency situation.

In the unlikely event that the song doesn't connect, the group makes it work by weaving it into the pattern. This is a chance for the other players to show their confidence in their fellow improviser's idea, trusting that it must be brilliant. If the group treats each of its players as a creative genius, they will be.

The Hot Spot is a high-energy game that's easy to learn, and as much fun to watch as it is to play.

KEY POINTS FOR CHAPTER THREE

*Respect choices made by others.

*There are no bad ideas.

*There are no mistakes. Everything is justified.

*Treat others as if they are poets, geniuses and artists, and they will be.

*The best way to look good is to make your fellow players look good.

CHAPTER FOUR
Agreement

Conflict is about as necessary as the Mad Scientist's daughter in a science fiction film. It's an arbitrary convention that need not be respected.

In the early days of improvisation, the molders and shapers of the art discovered very quickly that arguing on stage accomplished little, except to delay the action that would have naturally arisen in the first place.

"While improvising scenario plays at the Compass Theater, we discovered that when actors would go on stage, given the choice of agreeing or arguing, they would *inevitably* argue," observes Del. "Consequently, a scenario would last six or seven hours!

" 'Hand me the wrench.'

" 'I don't have it.'

" 'Go get it.'

" 'I don't know where it is.'

" 'It's in the car.'

" 'I don't want to go to the car.'

" 'But I need the wrench.'

" 'Then go get it.'

". . . And on and on. What would happen if we *agreed* instead of disagreed? Problems would be solved, and there would be more action — 'Here's the wrench, and I'll hold the light for you.'

"Business is taken care of in a lot less time! Freud, in his essay 'Psychopathic Characters on Stage,' called *Hamlet* the first truly modern play, because the conflict is not so much between the characters as *within* the characters.

"It's too easy to find ways to disagree. It strikes me that a more interesting thing for the art form — and for the planet —

is to look for ways to agree, rather than disagree. At the Improv-Olympic, the principle of agreement is taken even further by the 'Yes, & . . .' approach."

This is, in fact, a major difference between improv and scripted material. Much of drama is based on conflict, but when a playwright is devising the script, the arguments do more than delay action. Performers like Laurel and Hardy could probably perform the exchange about the wrench as written and have audiences rolling in the aisles because of the familiar interactions of their characters, but during an improv, such bickering only delays the furtherance of action.

In the hands of a writer, a disagreement can reveal hidden aspects of characters, aim the scene in a new direction, or convey other valuable information. When two improvisers are on stage arguing, they are only preventing something more interesting from happening.

Fortunately, there is a very simple way for even a first-time player to promote agreement.

YES, & . . .

"Yes, & . . ." is the most important rule in improvisation (the corporate name for the ImprovOlympic is "Yes & . . . Productions"). By following this simple rule, two players can build a scene before they know it.

The "Yes, & . . ." rule simply means that whenever two actors are on stage, they agree with each other to the Nth degree. If one asks the other a question, the other must respond positively, and then provide additional information, no matter how small: "Yes, you're right, and I also think we should . . ." Answering "No" leads nowhere in a scene:

A: Do you want to go to the movies?
B: No.

Even a positive answer is insufficient:

A: Do you want to go to the movies?
B: Yes.

The "Yes, & . . ." rule will lead players to their scene:

A: Do you want to go to the movies?

B: Yes, and let's go off our diets and eat a lot of greasy popcorn.

OR

B: Yes, let's sneak out of the house through the basement.

OR

B: Yes — is anybody picketing anything? I feel like counter-protesting.

With "Yes, & . . ." there are an unlimited number of scenic possibilities, and each player continues to supply information.

In this way, one step at a time, each player provides a building block, until they have easily, painlessly, constructed a scene. Answering "Yes, but . . ." stops any continued growth, while a flat "No" erases the block that has just been established.

Construction metaphors aside, this is a very relaxing way in which to work. A player knows that anything he says on stage will be immediately accepted by his fellow player, and treated as if it were the most scintillating idea ever offered to mankind. His partner then adds on to his idea, and moment by moment, the two of them have created a scene that neither of them had planned.

Agreement is the one rule that can never be broken: the players must be in agreement to forward the action of the scene.

When improvisers meet on stage, they agree to accept each other's initiations; they must completely commit to the reality they create for each other without a moment's hesitation. No matter how much of an improv cliché the line has become, if the first player says, "Well, here we are in Spain," then everyone on stage accepts that they are indeed in Spain. The next player might say, "Look out for that bull," and everyone *is* in the path of a charging bull. And so the scene is built.

Each new initiation furthers the last one, and the scene progresses. The acceptance of each other's ideas brings the players together, and engenders a "group mind." Denying the reality that is created on stage ends the progression of the scene, and destroys any chance of achieving a group consciousness.

Denials are taboo in improvisation. Being a good team player means having ethics. One of the best examples of denial in improv occurred during the early days of Second City, when Del and Joan Rivers were in the same company, and it rankles him to this day.

One night during an improvised scene, Joan told Del that she wanted a divorce. Del responded as an emotionally distraught husband might, in the hope of getting her to reconsider. "But honey, what about the children?" She replied, "We don't have any children!"

Naturally, she got a huge laugh. Naturally, she had completely destroyed the scene.

Rivers' laugh was at the expense of the scene, and she lost the trust of a fellow player. Her reply was a blatant denial of Del's initiation that they had children.

(In fairness, it must be noted that Miss Rivers was capable of brilliant scenic improvisation — Joan Rivers is certainly a talented, successful stand-up comic, but stand-up comedy is worlds apart from ensemble work.)

What kind of an improviser goes for the quick joke at the expense of his partner and the scene? Usually someone who is weak, insecure, or egotistical. It is an act of desperation, done to control the scene or to try and look better. A player who chooses this road finds few players will work with him on stage, because they know they will be sacrificed for an easy joke.

When an audience watches improvisers setting each other up with information, supporting each other's ideas, and furthering the scenes, they see true art in action.

Agreement

So far, this chapter has devoted itself to the importance of agreement and avoiding conflict. At the risk of confusion, there are ways in which an argument can be presented during an improvised scene.

While disagreement is not interesting, the *tension* that conflict causes may be. The players can agree to disagree (thus turning it into a game), as long as there is agreement between the players to further the scene. For example, a boxing match is not conflict. It *is* a fight, but it's actually a game played under an agreed-upon set of rules. Conflict in a scene between the *characters* may be used, but the conflict between the *players* must be avoided.

One of the finest examples of agreeing to disagree is the Monty Python "Argument Sketch," in which a man enters a room and finds another man at a desk:

"Is this the right room for an argument?"

"I've told you once."

"No you haven't."

"Yes I have."

"When?"

"Just now."

"No you didn't."

"Yes I did."

"Didn't."

"Did."

"Didn't."

"I'm telling you I did."

"You did not!"

"I'm sorry, is this a five-minute argument, or the full half-hour?"

. . . And it continues on into a hilarious argument. Obviously the scene is tightly scripted, rather than improvised on stage, but there is a clear-cut game at its core. It uses what appears to be conflict, but is actually total agreement, to forward the scene through a disagreement game.

GAMES TO TEACH AGREEMENT

Conflict Scenes

One of the first principles taught to students at the ImprovOlympia is that agreement is much more interesting than conflict.

This is done by placing the actors in situations which normally cause conflict on stage. However, they are instructed to make unusual choices, so that the expected conflict will not arise. These unlikely choices lead the scenes in interesting directions that could not have been planned.

However, this exercise is *not* about conflict. It is actually about agreement, and what develops after agreement is reached.

Conflict is merely the starting point, which leads the players to discover what the scene is about. It is the *relationship between the players* that makes the scene.

Possible conflict scenes might include "The Arrest," "The Robbery," or even "The Last Seat on the Bus." One example of a conflict scene leading into an interesting relationship was "The Robbery."

(A woman enters and finds a man in her home.)

WOMAN: Excuse me, what are you doing in my house?

MAN: I'm robbing you.

WOMAN: I don't know that I would have anything that you would want.

MAN: Well, these paintings are exquisite! I can tell they're not originals, but they are worth something.

WOMAN: Thank you. I painted those.

MAN: What? I am impressed! This is incredible work!

WOMAN: I am so flattered — I insist you have it.

As the relationship grows, they continue to share their expertise in the field of art, while she assists him in taking her prized possessions.

Another example of a conflict scene was done by Adam and Rick, portraying a cop chasing a robber. Both actors were running in place, giving the illusion of an officer chasing a thief:

COP: *(Panting)* Hey — I'm 50 years old and a little overweight. Can we stop and rest for a minute?

ROBBER: *(Panting)* You're not gonna grab me if we rest?

COP: Promise. Just for a few seconds — on the count of three. One, Two. Three.

(Both stop, heavily panting.)

COP: Boy, this part of my job is murder.

ROBBER: It's my least favorite part, too. But, it comes with the territory. Speaking of territory — this is a pretty tough beat for a 50-year-old.

COP: Yes. Well, experience counts for something. I'm ready — how about you?

ROBBER: Okay. One. Two. Three — go.

(Both start running.)

This scene continued on with the officer and the robber agreeing to stop every few beats, which allowed them to build an interesting relationship — proving once again that agreement in a potentially conflictive situation leads to an unusual choice!

The actors quickly discover that the audience laughs at agreement — a secret of comedy that very few people realize. Audiences aren't used to seeing actors agreeing very often, and they rarely see people agree to the things improv forces them to agree with!

Audiences at the ImprovOlympic have become quite sophisticated through the years. They respond poorly when they see denials on stage — and a few players are even booed!

The Ad Game

This game is a Del Close Special. It teaches several lessons, but it's particularly useful for actors to learn the "Yes, & . . ." approach to creating.

Usually played with approximately six or eight actors, the group has five minutes to create an ad campaign for an ordinary product with an unusual quality. For example: cereal that plays music when milk is poured on it.

The group must come up with a name for the product, a package design, a slogan, a spokesperson, and a jingle to create an entire marketing strategy and finished commercial.

Naturally, the only way to do this in five minutes is through complete and total agreement — no negative thinking is allowed. Every idea is accepted enthusiastically and remembered, each step is built off the previous idea. In order to properly brainwash the actors with this theory of acceptance, the director may want to force them to over-accept, screaming "Yes!" "Terrific idea!" "Great!" and other praises of brilliance after each idea is stated. This over-acceptance — particularly of stupid ideas — only makes the game funnier.

Most of the time, the players dramatize the game with lots of pacing, thinking, and enthusiastic shouts of agreement.

The Ad Game also familiarizes actors with important techniques for successfully creating a scene. The first, and most important, is the "Yes, & . . ." principle.

Everything is accepted, treated respectfully and, most importantly, *used*. The other players treat all ideas as if they were their own, and take turns building on them. There is an unspoken agreement between improvisers on stage: "You bring a brick, and I bring a brick. Then together, we build a house. You wouldn't bring in your own entire house and slap it on top of mine. Together, moment by moment, we create a scene."

Since every idea is remembered and used, players shouldn't give more than one suggestion for each topic. One is enough; the first one is always accepted and used — once the product is named, suggesting a second name takes the game sideways. The Ad Game teaches players to go forward. There's no need for a second suggestion, since the group will make the first suggestion work splendidly. In the Ad Game, the word "or" should never be used.

Since all of the workshop exercises are techniques for performance, they inevitably end up on stage in some form or another in Harolds (Of course, sometimes games are slightly amended in a performance situation for a particular Harold theme).

The following game was created by workshop students, based on the suggestion of a dog food that makes dogs talk (These students were clearly trying to test the theory that any idea will succeed).

AD EXECUTIVE: We have dog food that makes dogs talk. Now, who are we going to market this to?

RESPONSE: Lonely singles.

(All agree emphatically.)

AD EXEC: Okay, we need a name.

RESPONSE: Dinner Companion Dog Food.

(Shouts of approval)

AD EXEC: Great! We need a slogan.

RESPONSE: How about "When you're lonely, feed your dog?"

(Group praise)

AD EXEC: *(Repeating all suggestions so far, so that all is remembered)* Okay! Dinner Companion

Truth in Comedy

Dog Food. "When you're lonely, feed your dog." Hmmm ... how are we going to market this?

RESPONSE: TV!

AD EXEC: Yes! Now, who should we get as spokesperson for this type of product?

RESPONSE: How about the perfect conversationalist — Barbara Walters?

(Screams of delight)

AD EXEC: Perfect! What's this commercial going to look like?

RESPONSE: I see a candlelight dinner for two. A beautiful table exquisitely set.

OTHERS JOIN IN: And between the two candelabras is a gleaming silver can opener!

— Yes! Seated at the table are Barbara Walters and her dog!

— She is, of course, asking the dog a lot of very personal questions ...

— Which he answers with charm and wit!

AD EXEC: Wonderful! Is there music playing?

RESPONSE: Yes! Violin playing "Talk to Me, Like Lovers Do."

ANOTHER PLAYER: The label of the can will have a picture of a dog dressed in a suit and tie, with a boutonniere in his lapel and bouquet of roses tucked under his paw.

AD EXEC: And above that, the words "Dinner Companion. When you're lonely, feed your dog."

Another example was an Ad Game played during a Harold with the theme of "advertising." The Ad Game was used to show the important role advertising has played throughout history.

The scene takes place between Jesus and his disciples in a

brainstorming session for ideas to enhance the number of Jesus' followers. They immediately agree that rumors of a couple of miracles would be helpful, and agree to say that his mother was a virgin (although some resist this idea, thinking it too unbelievable).

Judas has an idea for a jingle. He sings "Silent Night, Holy Night/We're gonna rock around the clock tonight."

All the other disciples laugh and chide him for his musical ideas, especially his earlier suggestion for a musical play called "Godspell." He becomes angry and storms out. Trying in vain to get Judas to return, Jesus calls out to him, "Come on, Judas, turn the other cheek!"

Peter seizes this opportunity to use Jesus' statement as their new slogan. "After all," he says, "It's so much easier to understand than 'It is easier for a camel to get through the eye of a needle than for a rich man to get to heaven'."

All the disciples agree.

Now a spokesperson is needed. Simon shouts, "John the Baptist!"

"Yes," all agree. "There's a man with a head on his shoulders." (The audience groans here set off the Joke Alarm, warning the players not to get too "jokey.")

In heavy thought, Jesus paces back and forth across the room. He says, "We still need something else. Something *big* that will sell the crowd."

Meanwhile, the waitress begins removing the dinner dishes from the table. Noticing that Jesus' plate is still full, she asks, "Is he finished, or is he coming back?"

In unison, the disciples scream with delight, "HE'S COMING BACK!"

Using the basic idea of the Ad Game, the players rewrote biblical history.

KEY POINTS FOR CHAPTER FOUR

*Yes, and . . . Accept and build.

CHAPTER FIVE
Initiations and Game Moves

Giving Gifts

Improvisation is like steering a car by looking through the rear view mirror, according to British director Keith Johnstone. You don't know where you're going, you can only see where you've been.

When two improvisers step on stage, neither one should know anything about the scene they are about to create — they basically start with nothing.

In improvisation, an initiation is the first information provided by one of the players. This can be a line of dialog, a gesture, or even an attitude.

A good initiation is vital to the scene, because it provides players with information that forms the foundation of their scene. The best initiations make assumptions, usually about their relationship, roles, or locations. Naturally, the other player accepts, embraces and builds on whatever is offered in that initiation, so the scene will be off to a rousing start.

A scene that begins with one player saying "Hello" to the other generally indicates a slow start, while a line like "Guten morgen, Herr Doctor, your experiment is on the slab" offers all sorts of potential to a fellow improviser.

Whatever the initiation may be, the players then take turns adding information. They'll soon discover that they've built a scene through their responses to each other's initiations.

He who gives information is a gift-giver; he who asks questions is a thief.

Questions — asking other players for information — are an unnecessary evil for improvisers. Instead of providing fellow actors with facts, questions place the burden of invention upon the other players. It's much better for an improviser to *assume* he knows the same information as the other actors, and use the opportunity to contribute his own share of information to the scene.

When a player asks a question, he usually has an answer in mind. So, why ask the question in the first place? If he wants to bring a particular idea into the scene, phrasing it as a question is usually a bad move. After all, his fellow player may not have the same idea that he does, and he may get a completely different answer than he had hoped for.

When two actors in a workshop were portraying a homeless couple, the wife had the idea to find a lottery ticket in the street. Unfortunately, her husband didn't know this, so when she pointed to the ground and said, "Look, what's that?", the husband replied, "Uh . . . it's just a pile of shit."

The woman was flustered. "No," she said, completely denying his on-the-spot assumption. "It's a lottery ticket."

Wrong! It *was* a pile of shit. It *would* have been a lottery ticket, if only she had said so in the first place!

Of course, some questions are worse than others; some questions provide information, rather than require it. Asking, "Look, what's that?" is much less helpful than, "Look, is that a lottery ticket?" Of course, it's easier to simply say, "Look, there's a lottery ticket."

GAME MOVES IN SCENES

People are natural game players.

Some of the games are obvious, like *Monopoly, Trivial Pursuit,* and baseball. Dr. Eric Berne's book *Games People Play* deals with more subtle, psychological, interpersonal games that people play to get what they want out of a specific relationship.

Likewise, improvisers initiate game moves to indicate the types of games being played in a scene. The game provides the structure needed to solve the problem of the scene.

Initiations and Game Moves

The games, or scenic structures, are always created on the spot as part of the improvised initiation. Picking up on the game move separates good game players from those who don't pay attention. When an actor discovers what his fellow improviser wants, he should, by all means, give it to him!

Some scenic games (games that develop in the context of a scene, as opposed to those performed as the result of a deliberate decision) are standard, easily taught techniques, like one-upmanship or speaking in verse, while others are invented on the spot.

Most of the time, the scenic game is discovered within the first three lines of the scene. When it is missed, it's usually because the players haven't paid close attention.

Film and television comedy are filled with scenic games. The Marx Brothers' "Stateroom Scene" from *A Night at the Opera* is really a game of "How Many People Can We Cram Into This Tiny Room?" *I Love Lucy* usually involved a game of "Try to Sneak Into Ricky's Act." In their slapstick films, Laurel and Hardy generally played a game that critics refer to as "Reciprocal Destruction," which is just what it sounds like.

Even Monty Python's "Argument Sketch," like the majority of their sketches, is a good example of a scenic game. If it was an improvised scene, a player would have no trouble discovering the game to play from the first three lines:

"Is this the right room for an argument?"

(Even though this is a question, it is loaded with information and clear intent to play a game.)

"I've told you once."

"No you haven't."

The game, or structure of the scene, is already crystal clear from those lines alone, and any experienced improvisers could step in here and keep it going.

When an improviser finds the game within a scene, he's found the scene, and that's why it's so important to pick up on any possible game moves. If a game move is clear-cut, it can excuse almost anything — as actor George Segal told Del, "Even if you're five minutes into a scene, it's not too late to put on a foreign accent!"

Another good example of a game being discovered in a scene occurred during a workshop involving six players. One of them was to receive a huge promotion from the company president, and they waited anxiously in a conference room for the decision to be announced.

PETE: My son is on a kidney dialysis machine. *(An obvious sympathy ploy)*

JENNA: And you're not with him?

PETE: No, I had to be here today.

JENNA: Oh, you should be with him every second. At times like these, a child needs a father. *(The others all agree, increasing Pete's guilt.)*

PETE: You're right. I'm going to him now. Thanks, guys. *(He hugs the others and exits.)*

DENNIS: Thank goodness my kid is healthy.

JENNA: Is he?

DENNIS: Yes, and athletic. A little league baseball player.

JENNA: Does he play in little league games after school?

DENNIS: Yes, he's pitching today.

JENNA: And you're not there?

DENNIS: Why, no. I had to be here.

PAT: When I was a boy, my dad never watched me play. I once pitched a no-hitter, and he missed it. I never forgave him.

(Others chime in, once again indicating Dennis is neglecting his son, jeopardizing their relationship.)

DENNIS: You're right. My son is only young once.

What's more important than my son? I'm going to him. Thanks, guys.

(Dennis exits. The others look around at each other, sensing fully their intent to get rid of each other.)

JENNA: *(Relieved)* I have no kids. Nowhere to go, nothing to do.

PAT: That explains that nice tan. Plenty of time to lie in the sun and pamper yourself on the weekend.

JENNA: Yes.

PAT: That's a cute little mole on your arm. Probably from the sun.

MARK: Sounds like something that could develop into cancer. I knew someone who had a mole just like that, may she rest in peace. The sun is very dangerous.

PAT: You should have that checked immediately.

JENNA: It's just a little mole. Do you really think I should worry?

PAT: What's more important than your health?

JENNA: You're right. I'd better go. Thanks, guys. *(She exits. There are just three men left.)*

PAT: Can you believe it? Twenty-seven million dollars in the lottery. Did you guys get your tickets yet?

MARK: Yep.

BILL: No. But I've been playing the same number every single day for a year and I never win. I'm not too worried about missing this one day.

PAT: What's the matter, Bill? Trying to prove to yourself that you're not addicted?

BILL: *(Nervously)* No.

MARK: I knew a guy who always played the same number for years. Then, one day, he was too busy to buy a ticket, and sure enough, that was the day his number was drawn. He missed his chance. Boy, he wanted to kill himself.

PAT: Twenty-seven million, Bill.

BILL: I gotta get a ticket, quick! *(He runs out, Pat and Mark eye each other carefully.)*

MARK: Isn't that your car alarm?

This game of manipulating each other out of the room was established in the very first exchange between Jenna and Pete; all the others observed it, and skillfully played it out.

Another example of finding a game in the scene was done by a house team called The Family. They were doing a Harold with the theme of "Santa." Throughout the Harold, they performed monologs giving statistics about the homeless and the increasing suicide rate at Christmas. In their last scene, they found a game to illustrate how depressing Christmas is. As a group, they began singing Christmas carols. During the first verse of "Jingle Bells," Adam took an imaginary gun and shot himself in the head, then fell on the stage.

The others stared briefly and began to sing "The First Noel." During the first verse, Miles pretended to hang himself from a noose. The others cut him down, and his body fell next to Adam. The survivors began to sing "Rudolph, the Red Nosed Reindeer." One by one, they continued to play the game of "committing suicide." Finally, with a pile of bodies next to her, Rachael began singing, softly and beautifully, "Silent Night." On the last line, she pointed to the heap of bodies and sang "Sleep in heavenly peace" to end the game.

Another example of finding the game within the scene is a one-upmanship game Charna discovered in a scene with Scott.

The scene established that they had been dieting for days, when the pair sat down to their three ounces of protein and one cup of vegetables. Scott took a slice of bread. Charna scolded him, because he'd eaten his daily serving of bread at breakfast. To spite her, Scott took the bread and put a whole stick of butter on it, topped with a second slice of bread.

To retaliate, Charna put four teaspoons of sugar in her coffee. Scott picked up the sugar bowl and poured it into his mouth. Charna ran to the refrigerator to get the cake she baked for their party, and began shoving fistfuls of it into her mouth. The food war game escalated until it could build no more.

LISTENING AND RESPONDING

Hearing and listening are two different things. When a player is given an initiation, he must let the words resonate inside his head for a moment, so that he can decipher the underlying meaning.

An improviser must consider what is said, and what is left unsaid, as well. He must think, "Why was that said? What does she mean by that? How does it make me feel?"

If a player takes the time to consider what the other speaker means, then his response is more intelligent than the knee-jerk response (usually a one-liner that attempts to be witty). A more carefully considered response takes a second or two longer, but the wait is well worthwhile.

A player's move is not complete until he sees how it affects his partner. When his line has been heard and pondered, his fellow player then responds from a similarly honest and emotional state.

Some of the very best improvisers are those that listen and remember. Former ImprovOlympic player Chris Farley is an expert at this rule, both on and off the stage. Chris listens with his emotions; his fellow players can see him responding while they are still saying their lines. And he never forgets a thing that is said.

Charna says Chris still reminds her of something she said or did years ago, which is why she finds "The Chris Farley Show" on *Saturday Night Live* so funny. Chris interviews show business giants by reminding them of his favorite moments from their films, saying "Remember when you did this . . . That was awesome . . ." Hosting his own talk show, he never asks questions — he just remembers! The *SNL* writers are very obviously heightening one of Chris' natural traits. He remembers everything!

AVOIDING PRECONCEIVED NOTIONS

Preconceived ideas for an improv scene can get a player into trouble.

==Avoiding preconceptions is as easy as listening and using each other's initiations.==

Of course, a previous scene may give an actor a notion for a location, relationship, or a situation. However, his grasp on such a thought must be loose, and dropped quickly if the scene takes a turn that contradicts his plans.

For example, Madeline might enter a scene with the intention of being Dave's long lost lover. She begins by saying, "I've missed you terribly." If Dave responds by saying, "I know. Sorry I haven't written, Mom," then Madeline must immediately discard her romantic scenario.

Of course, it's important to remember that initiations can be nonverbal, as well as verbal. The way an initiation is presented is just as important as the words themselves, and the accomplished improviser must always be listening for intonations and hidden meanings. If Madeline's opening line was spoken with sexual innuendo, then Dave would have turned it into an incestuous love scene, which would probably lead to the discovery of why the boy left home in the first place.

One last comment on listening: always listen to the whole idea in a statement. When a player is cut off in the middle of a sentence, his fellow players cannot respond to the best of their ability until the entire statement has been made. It's just simple logic.

As Del once said during a conversation with Charna's mother, "Cut off the comedian and you miss the punchline!"

EXERCISES

Freeze Tag

Freeze Tag, sometimes known as "Switch," is a simple way to work on initiations. Two people begin a scene with dialog and a physical activity. A third player shouts "Freeze!" to stop the action, and the improvisers immediately stop in midscene.

When the players are "frozen," the third player will tag one of them out and take his place in the same physical position. He then starts an entirely new and different scene which justifies the physical positions of both players. In the opening line of each new scene, the initiation must be clear, so the new scene is immediately understood.

The following is an example of how a Freeze Tag might look. If the opening line, taken from the audience, is "Let me carry you over the threshold," the exercise could begin with a woman carrying a man in her arms (knowing how players take unusual choices):

WOMAN: Let me carry you over the threshold.

MAN: You are such a feminist.

FREEZE!

Players are frozen while a second man tags out the woman, trading places with her. He takes the exact position, holding the first man in his arms. Since he has entered, it is up to him to deliver the first line:

2ND MAN: You're lucky I caught you falling from that high-rise, Jimmy!

MAN: Golly gee, Superman, it's a good thing you were flying by.

(Superman puts Jimmy down, and puts his hands on his hips.)

FREEZE!

Another player taps the man playing Jimmy, who was

standing with his arms at his sides, looking at Superman. She assumes Jimmy's position and speaks:

> NEW WOMAN: Simon didn't say, "Put your hands on your hips." You're out!
>
> 2ND MAN: Oh, give me one more chance!
>
> NEW WOMAN: Okay. Simon says, "Lay face down on the floor." *(He does.)*
>
> FREEZE!

A player tags the standing woman, and looks down at the man on the floor, and says, "Last call!"

The game goes on as long as the director, the audience, or the players choose. In our shoes, the scenes return a few times to make connections, so the game may go on as long as ten minutes. In the example on the preceding page, Superman could return intermittently throughout the freeze tag.

Three-Line Scenes

In this exercise, two players must discover a scene in only three lines of dialog. Obviously, this is a good way to teach them to say exactly what needs to be said as clearly as possible — in other words, to be concise.

Since a scene — even a three-line scene — has limitless possibilities, this exercise is sometimes played by making the group do a number of three-line scenes that all begin with the same first line. It quickly becomes clear that the second person can put an entirely different spin on the first sentence. In fact, the second line can be the most important of the three.

This exercise also enhances listening skills. The emotion behind a line reading can change its entire meaning, and so it's easy for very different scenes to result from the same opening line.

Three-line scenes teach a player how to add, as it is used in "Yes, & . . ." Agreeing with the opening line won't advance the scene or provide any new information to build a scene together. Contributing something else gives extra meaning to the opening line, and helps create a scene.

Example of agreement:

"Here is a mango."

"Oh, good!"

Example of agreement (and adding "Yes, and . . ."):

"Here is a mango."

"Oh, good! At least we know there's food on this deserted island!"

Quite a difference, eh? And when exactly three lines are

allowed to create a scene, progress has to be made quickly. As we see in the latter example, the second line adds new information and raises the stakes.

Here are some more examples of three-line scenes where each line adds a piece of information. We'll use the same first line to prove how the scene changes as it's built; this illustrates how actors cannot assume they know what the scene is about simply by hearing the first line.

PLAYER ONE: Sign here.

PLAY TWO: This makes it official.

PLAYER ONE: Yes, we're now legally divorced.

Player Two takes what might have been the act of signing for a delivery and makes it much more important by adding, "This makes it official." Suddenly the idea changed; it was no longer a delivery sheet, but an official document. The first player adds to the idea by making it a divorce decree, and the scene is clearly under way. A different response by Player Two would have resulted in a very different scene, as shown by the following:

PLAYER ONE: Sign here.

PLAYER TWO: I've never been asked to autograph a woman's chest before.

PLAYER ONE: Well, I'm your biggest fan!

From that same opening line, the players discover a relationship between a star and his fan.

It is vital to listen to the emotional tone which provides the underlying meaning behind the spoken words. This subtext *must* be heeded! The words may sound positive, but the emotional tone can indicate otherwise, as is seen in this example:

CHRIS: I've had another unsuccessful day of job hunting.

STUART: Why don't you read some of my self-help books?

CHRIS: Sometimes I feel like murdering you in your sleep.

Reading these words in cold type, it appears Stuart is trying to be helpful to Chris. But Chris paid close attention to Stuart's smug attitude, and responded correctly!

Tim Kazurinski of *Saturday Night Live* recalls that while he was at Second City, Del would drill them over and over with three-line scenes.

"When you were on stage, you said the opening line, the person who jumped up on stage said another line, and you had to respond. That meant that in those three lines, you had to identify who you were, where you were, and what this scene could be about. We quickly learned to identify the who, the what, the where and the why in three lines," says Kazurinski. "Then, you left the stage, and the person who only had the one line stayed on stage. Another person entered, and another scene started.

"It was like the nuns that drilled me on my times tables back in school. It was just brutal, but I learned my times tables and my scenes! Del had us do these things time and time again until we had the point in our heads — get in there, get it done, don't do 'here we are in Spain.'

"When he was working us, he knew just the right exercises to break us out of our rut. There were times when we would come to class when Del had drifted off or wandered or jabbered too much, but when you came the next time and he was on, he could say things to whip an entire class into a frenzy. We were so focused, there were doors slamming open in our minds and shafts of light streaming in. We would go, '*That's* what it's about! *That's* how to do it! *That's* why I'm here!' He would jump you and get your ass up on stage and work you, and it would become so clear as to what it was all about. He's one of the true geniuses I've ever met."

KEY POINTS FOR CHAPTER FIVE

*Make assumptions — don't ask questions.
*Look for the game within your scene and play it.
*Listen and remember.
*Listen for the whole idea in a statement.
*Avoid preconceived notions.

CHAPTER SIX
Moment to Moment to Moment

Life is what happens to you while you're busy making other plans.

— *John Lennon*

The games of ping pong and chess require very different strategies.

Chess players must plan many moves ahead, and players concentrate on pushing their own moves forward, despite the designs of their opponents.

In addition to being a physical game, players cannot plan ahead in ping pong; they have to react in a split second.

One player cannot "pong" until his opponent has "pinged." He can aim his return shot, and even try to anticipate the next volley, but ultimately he has to focus his attention on where the ball actually lands on his side of the table.

Unlike a chess player, he cannot be thinking several moves ahead — he has to pay attention to that moment. And that moment leads directly to future moments.

Improv is much closer to ping pong than it is to chess. Actors create an improv scene in the same spontaneous way.

An actor following each moment through to the next is constantly making discoveries, an ideal state for improvisers. If a player is planning ahead and thinking about the direction he wants the action to go, then he isn't paying attention to what is going on at the moment. Unfortunately for him and his fellow actors, what is going on at the moment is the scene!

This is a mistake that happens all too often, and may even occur with an experienced performer. When he thinks he sees where a scene is headed, he may steer it that way, without paying careful attention to what is happening on stage at that moment. He's living for the possible future of the scene at the expense of the present.

Unless it is part of a game move, improvisers should resist trying to fulfill the audience's expectations, says George Wendt of *Cheers*; fortunately this is easier in improv than for performers trying to develop material further.

"Always assume the audience is one step ahead of you," he says, quoting one of the most useful rules he learned while working with Del.

In improv, you almost never give the audience what they're expecting, because you're working on the fly — this really relates more to shaping the material.

"Always assume that the audience is going to get the easy joke. In other words, if an audience sees a set-up coming, they're less likely to laugh at the joke. If they see a set-up coming, you'd better do a quick 180 and give them something that they don't expect," he says.

"This dates back to the audiences that defined the Compass Players and the original Second City folks, audiences that were truly one step ahead of everyone else, that highly intellectual beatnik literati sort of coffeehouse crowd. But it holds true."

Wendt says the principle has also proven true in his television work.

"The concept of respect for audiences holds true in the most successful comedies, and I'll lump *Cheers* in with that. I think *Cheers* is quite clever, and a large part of the success of *Cheers* is due to a basic respect for the audience. I understand that in writing sessions, if two writers think of the same joke at the same time, they throw it out. Too easy. It has many corollaries, but I think you should always assume that the audience is one step ahead of you."

There's certainly nothing wrong with a prepared Harold performer, as long as the actor is willing to drop his preconceptions immediately.

For example, two actors are on stage talking about ordering a pizza, when a third player decides to enter the scene as a pizza delivery man. If one of the actors greets him with, "I see the new manhole covers have arrived," then his pizzas have *immediately* turned into manhole covers. He must be light enough on his feet to spring from moment to moment, according to the needs of the scene, no matter how brilliant his own ideas may be (or how little sense he thinks the other actors are making).

The only appropriate response the actor bearing the pizzas-turned-manhole covers can then make is, "Yes, here are your new manhole covers, *and . . .*," with the actor making one of countless thousands of choices to continue the action.

If something unusual or unexpected occurs, an inexperienced actor sometimes ignores it, thinking it isn't important because it's not in line with what he thinks should be happening. *Wrong!* The actor entering the scene, the audience, and even the other actor may all be expecting a pizza — indeed, it's probably the most appropriate move — but if one actor decides the man is delivering manhole covers, then he is right, and everyone must immediately accept it.

Everyone might initially view this as a mistake, but the only true mistake is for the other actors to ignore or negate him, and turn manhole covers back into a pizza. So the actors must justify the line, and can only do so by being *in the moment*. Remember, if everyone justifies everyone else's actions, there are no mistakes.

That unexpected line could be the interesting twist that shapes the scene right before the players' eyes. The pizza delivery is appropriate and expected, but the arrival of a person with manhole covers is guaranteed to make the scene more interesting!

After all, a scene is almost never about what the players think it's going to be about. Once underway, the actors follow the scene along, but they shouldn't try to control it. The scene

Truth in Comedy

is the result of the relationship between the characters, and the relationship that grows from those explored moments.

==Nothing is ignored.==

==Nothing is forgotten.==

==And nothing is a "mistake==."

THE REASON WHY

Since one of the most important responsibilities of an improviser is justifying what his fellow players say and do, everything that happens on stage is used to build the scenes — so there *can't* be mistakes if it's all accepted.

Of course, not everything needs to be justified immediately. Everything heard should be remembered and eventually used; the players will make sense out of it before the scene is over. One of the primary uses of discovery is finding how some seemingly confusing element introduced early in a scene (and apparently forgotten) is found to have a vital place in the denouement.

One of the surest audience-pleasers in an improv scene is also one of the easiest to accomplish. A crowd delights in seeing a player pull out a forgotten scenic element just in time to solve a problem — like a chess player suddenly executing a checkmate, apparently out of nowhere.

An example of delayed justification is a scene between Mary and Robin. Mary looks over her doll collection, while Robin is sitting at a desk, engrossed in figuring out bills.

MARY: "I can't figure out why I keep finding the heads torn off my dolls."

ROBIN: "You owe me fifty dollars for the phone bill."

MARY: "I don't have the money for my share of the bill."

(The pair starts quarreling, until Robin gives up in frustration. Finally, she calmly walks over and

tears the head off a doll.)

The two of them were able to justify the opening line brilliantly (although the ending of the scene appears obvious on paper, it is something else entirely when the audience watches it being created). The scene was not about pulling the heads off dolls; it was about the frustrations of two roomates. In improvising the scene, the players discovered the past history of their relationship. The missing heads obviously indicate that Robin has been frustrated by her roommate in the past, and allows for some interesting possibilities if the scene is continued in the future.

An actor can only justify scenic moves — and any seeming "mistakes" — if he is "in the moment," and not planning ahead. Two easy exercises to help develop this are the Conducted Story and the One-Word Story.

ONE-WORD STORY

The One-Word Story is one of the simplest of all improv exercises, and very useful for teaching the importance of staying in the moment.

Here, a group of players (usually six to eight) build a story one word at a time. The basic method sees the actors line up on stage and, beginning at one end, each speaking one word, forming sentences and telling a story.

This is quite easy to do, assuming the players don't try to plan ahead, but more difficult to do smoothly and well. The words should come quickly, practically without thinking (though of course they should be sensible, coherent sentences), but the group should make it sound as if one person is telling a story at a normal, conversational pace.

One of the best ways to achieve this is by *listening* — paying attention to what is going on at the moment. It's impossible to think about what to say in advance, because one player can completely change direction, and a player who thinks before speaking only delays the story. The response should be reflexive rather than a carefully chosen word (this is in sharp contrast to scenes, where each response is slowly and carefully considered). The word "and" should also be avoided, and players must strive to sound like one voice.

As the group becomes more comfortable with the game, there are other devices to enhance its value. One variation has any player who delays in responding to step out of the group, eliminating the slower players one by one, as in a spelling bee; this teaches the group to keep up the pace. Naturally, inappropriate responses also cause players to lose (when played in front of a group or an audience, good-natured jeering often results). When a player fails, he is often forced to stage his own death before the audience and his teammates, preferably in some manner that reflects the story at that point. Another technique, particularly used in a performance (or as an opening exercise) utilizes a theme, a title, or an audience suggestion for the story.

CONDUCTED STORY

A Conducted Story is a little more elaborate than a One-Word Story, but the principle is the same. Like the One-Word Story, this teaches players the importance of being "in the moment," and makes it painfully obvious when they are not.

Basic Conducted Stories require players to build a story together, as though they had one brain, but several mouths. The players line up in a semicircle on stage, with one of them crouched down at the front of the group to function as a conductor, just as a symphony conductor leads an orchestra.

The conductor leads the narration — generally one player at a time — by pointing at (or otherwise signifying to) the players so they know when to start and stop talking. The exercise often begins with an audience choosing a title, or an object that eventually is incorporated into the story. The goal of the group is to tell one single, coherent story with short segments, as chosen by the conductor.

When the conductor points at a player, he begins speaking

immediately, picking up the tale precisely where the last player left off. He continues talking for as long as — or as short as — the conductor indicates. When the conductor suddenly points to someone else, the player shuts up instantly so that the new player can pick up the story from him.

The challenge for each improviser is picking up the very next word — or even the very next syllable — in the sentence. Each player has to listen carefully and watch the conductor at all times, so that he can stop on command. The story should not be choppy, but told in a continuous narrative voice.

During a scene, a beginning improviser often has trouble knowing when he is not in the moment. If he tries to think ahead during a Conducted Story, however, his mistake will stick out like a sore thumb. Players who think ahead trying to second-guess what comes next in the story usually end up starting a new sentence when they are pointed at, instead of finishing the sentence started by a fellow player. This is because the actor wasn't listening. The only way to succeed at a Conducted Story is to listen and pay attention every step of the way.

The pace of editing each narrator varies according to the whim of the conductor, but the Conducted Story is most entertaining when the players have to finish each other's thoughts.

In building the story, the players should be conscious of all of the necessary components that make a story interesting — elements like action, characters, emotion, ambiance, a cohesive story line and a resolution. It's important to tell the story as coherently as possible. Trying to make it silly or crazy often makes it less effective — since it's being created by several minds working together, it's guaranteed to get silly enough on its own. As a group, the players know that a resolution to their story is needed; with the common goal in mind, they will find it.

Various writing styles or points of view can be used to add dimension to the Conducted Story. Each player may narrate in the style of a different well-known author (often selected by an audience), while still committed to carrying the story forward.

One memorable narrated story was actually performed by an ImprovOlympic team comprised entirely of psychologists. Each of them assumed the point of view of a different mental illness! While telling the story together, they separately revealed the symptoms of a psychotic, a paranoid-schizophrenic, a manic-depressive, a hypochondriac, and several others.

There are other devices more experienced players can use for workshops or performance, involving similar techniques and principles which force players to stay in the moment, and not think ahead. Some practices have resulted in several people portraying one character in a scene, and the actors have to speak at a normal pace, *completely in unison* (it's actually easier than it may sound). Other workshops have devised oracles, which speak one word at a time to address (and answer!)

great philosophical questions of the universe.

KEY POINTS FOR CHAPTER SIX

*Stay in the moment. What is happening *now* will be the key to discovery.

*Nothing is ignored. Follow the unexpected twist.

*There is no such thing as a mistake.

CHAPTER SEVEN
Building a Scene

Action begins with the disruption of a routine.
— Keith Johnstone

WHAT IS A SCENE?

Two actors on stage do not make a scene.

A pair of performers standing before an audience, talking to each other about their mother-in-law problems, do not constitute a scene — they may just be having a jokey (if clichéd) discussion. Several improvisers doing a Pattern Game or Hot Spot may interact in a very entertaining manner, but they aren't doing a scene.

So then what *is* a scene?

Every scene contains a few key elements.

Most importantly, a *relationship* must exist between the characters on stage. In improv, it's normally discovered through the course of a scene; the more quickly it is found, the faster the scene progresses.

Of course, the easiest way to advance a scene is for the performers to make assumptions. If the first line is, "I've come for my test results, Doctor," we already have a fairly solid idea of the relationship. And if the response is, "You have a very peculiar disease, Mr. President," the relationship is clearly defined. There is enough information for a scene; the groundwork has been laid.

Also important is the relationship between the players and their *environment,* which is also discovered through improv. The scene between the President and the Doctor will be radically different if we discover it takes place in outer space rather than the Oval Office.

No matter what the setup, however, the *event* is crucial to every scene — *the situation that makes this day different from all the rest.* This is where the action begins. It arises from the game moves, which become the structure of the scene. It can arise from the very first sentence, or even before any words are spoken.

Many scenes don't start off as strongly or with as many assumptions as the previous example. Two actors walk on stage and may find themselves doing something more mundane or routine, such as washing dishes or tightening bolts in an assembly line. As the Keith Johnstone quote at the beginning of the chapter tells us, it is when the routine is disrupted that the action of the scene begins.

And what results is usually far more interesting than what was planned.

KEEPING AN OPEN MIND

There is a big difference between a strong, information-filled initiation that makes assumptions, and a preconceived notion used to control a scene.

For example, the opening exchange in the scene between the President and the Doctor starts out with an opening line and an assumption, but the player (presumably) isn't trying to promote a pre-planned scenario. If he was, the equally presumptuous response probably demolished any intended plot. The biggest mistake the first player could make would be to downplay his partner's response in order to continue shoving his scenario down the throat of his partner.

Having an idea is not bad in itself, especially if the actor conveys it easily to his partner through a simple initiation, such as a line of dialog or a physical movement. The simpler the idea, the better.

It is vitally important, however, for an improviser to drop his idea immediately the moment the scene takes an unexpected twist. Of course, it doesn't make much sense for one player to devise an elaborate plot for the scene.

When all the players are involved in its creation, the scene is much more interesting. Two heads are better than one, and in Harold, six or eight heads are even better.

A common mistake for some improvisers is to be led by the audience. If the crowd laughs loudly at one particular moment, the performer may be tempted to push the scene in the direction that the audience is responding to — instead of responding to his fellow performers.

Unfortunately, an audience doesn't necessarily want what it thinks it wants. A player is usually much better off listening to his fellow performers and director than the audience members. George Wendt remembers that during his days at Second City, it wasn't enough to make the crowd laugh.

"Del said, 'We don't care if it works for the audience — it has to work for us,'" says Wendt. "At that time, an improv scene that we may have become fond of because it got a lot of laughs had to work for Del, (producer) Bernie Sahlins, and (pianist) Fred Kaz — all three of them — or else it would not be considered for our Second City show. 'Don't tell us it works — we'll tell *you* if it works.'"

START IN THE MIDDLE

Exposition sucks.

Backstories and explanations are rarely the most exciting part of any book or film; generally they are a necessary evil.

In improvisation, actors are seldom hamstrung by exposition. Instead, they simply ignore it all, and begin their scenes in the middle!

Nothing is more boring or wastes more time than two improvisers starting a scene with "Who are you?" It is always helpful if the players know each other (or their roles) when they begin their scene; they need to make assumptions about their relationship right from the start.

When two players pretend their scene actually began five minutes before the lights went up, they make discoveries much more quickly. They spare the audience their excruciatingly dull groping around for information that should simply be assumed.

SHOW, DON'T TELL

An improviser accepts what his partner says as a gift, and builds on that idea. He may respond with another gift, and the two of them build their scene based on the information in their statements.

They must make *active* choices, rather than passive ones, and then follow through on their ideas. Everything said can be heard and used, even what might be considered a mistake. Since "action begins with the disruption of a routine," the "mistake" could be the disruption that begins the action.

Too many actors make the error of talking about doing something instead of doing it; a potentially interesting scene gets frittered away because no one is actually doing anything. If the idea is active, it leads, step by step, to the next idea. But if the idea is talked away, the actors never arrive at the next idea.

Suppose two actors are on stage, and one of them must choose whether to stay with his wife and children, or run off to a silver mine in South America. An inexperienced improviser might make the mistake of agonizing over the decision for several minutes, weighing the pros and cons. Boring! He might even choose to stay with his family. This is a more noble decision, but he's just chosen the routine, rather than the disruption, and we're left with no action. He's also wasted the audience's time wallowing in his angst. Chekov or Ibsen could probably script an interesting version of this scenario, but in improv, the active choice is the only one to take.

Given the choice, any experienced improviser must immediately leave his wife and family, and run off to South America. If it's only a thirty-second scene, so be it — this allows us more time for their follow-up scene, which will obviously begin deep in the South American silver mine. See how much further the active choice leads?

Scenes are much more interesting when the idea is seen, rather than *talked about*.

Active choices forward the scene.

Passive choices keep it stagnant.

There's really no choice, is there?

LISTENING FOR THE GAME

Careful players will note that the structure of any good scene is usually a game, one that is discovered in the first three lines of dialog.

A game doesn't have to be as specific and organized as some of the improv exercises explained throughout this book. Games are found within scenes. One example is one-upmanship, where each player tries topping the other with every sentence (and of course, the opposite — continuing to lower one's own status — is equally valid). There are countless other games that develop within scenes that have nothing to do with status. Players may find themselves saying the exact opposite of what they are thinking during the course of a scene; in another scene, the actors find an excuse to touch each other every time they speak (this is also a good exercise to teach physicality).

Howard recalls one ImprovOlympic performance attended by executives of Budweiser, who were there to decide whether they wanted to sponsor that year's playoffs. When the "Baron's Barracudas" team took the stage, sure enough, the suggestion for the improv was "beer." However, the players instantly discovered an outrageously successful game: they began mentioning different brand names of beer, all in a favorable context. At the conclusion of the scene, they burst into a room, saying it was filled with "the finest beers in the world." They rattled off the names of dozens of beers — none of them Budweiser — and the response grew with each successive beer.

By the end of the scene, the executives were on the floor laughing, and the name "Budweiser" had never been spoken. Thus, the players discovered the "Ignore Budweiser" game, which proved to be the most successful possible choice.

To discover the potential games in each scene, players must pay close attention from the start. They must be especially careful to notice their own lines, since players often aren't aware of the games they are setting up themselves. There is a part of the human brain that is very skilled at improvisation, and it is usually setting up a player's scenes for him (however subconsciously). So, he has to be careful not to get in the way of his own ideas!

When an actor pays the same attention to his own lines as he pays to clues in a murder mystery, he sees his scenes instantly. Unfortunately, players often let their egos get in the way. They think they have a funny idea, and that is what the scene *must* be about. While they plan what they think *should* be happening, they are ignoring what actually *is* happening.

Some improvisers are so busy searching for the scene, they don't notice it pass them by. However, if they force their egos out of the way and trust the choice made by the group, they'll all discover their scene together. They need to remember they are not playwrights — they are improvisers.

PATTERNS IN SCENES

Players must not only be alert to game moves, they must also be aware of the patterns in a scene — and then play them. For example, one way to end a scene is to return to the beginning of that same scene, whether through a line, a gesture, or a completed cycle. All of life follows a cycle, and improvisation is no different. The patterns become part of the scenic game. When the players recognize the patterns in a scene, they'll set each other up for game moves to forward that scene. And when they understand the game they set up for themselves, and play it full tilt, they've got it made!

Find your game, and you've found your scene.

Del is fond of the "group mind" concept that develops during improv when everything works, and the ability to wire human minds together to become "Supermen."

"We are releasing higher and greater powers of the human being," he explains. "That is what we mean when we say that Harold 'appears.' A melding of the brains occurs on stage. When improvisers are using seven or eight brains instead of just their own, they can do no wrong! Time slows down, and the player has a sense of where he is.

"I was talking with Gary Fencik of the Chicago Bears, and I asked him what it felt like when they were beating New York in the playoffs, on their way to winning the Super Bowl. He told me that he knew what everybody was doing and where they were. He had a complete holographic image in his mind, a three-dimensional picture of the field."

A similar event occurs during a successful improv. "On stage, one has a complete picture of what is going on, and also a clear sense of all potential moves. They are almost laid out in time. The pattern-making mechanism is kicked on, and yet, one's intellect does not desert him," explains Del.

"Somehow, the improviser is in the balanced right and left hemisphere state. He can almost see time as a dimension, as he can almost see his potential moves extend physically into the future. It's then very easy to decide which move to choose, and then go with it. Since everyone is on the same wavelength, each player sees what the other sees.

"It's an absolute thrill, a tremendous surge of confidence, energy, and joy. I've given up searching for happiness, now that I realize joy is very easily achieved!"

KEEPING ACTION IN THE PRESENT

There's little point in a player discussing the past or planning the future in a scene. A good improviser shows us the *now*. It's always much more interesting to see it, rather than hear about it. After all, this is a *visual* medium!

This also applies to actors discussing events that are happening off stage. If the audience is told that the most interesting action in a scene is occurring elsewhere, why should they care about the discussion they are seeing in front of them? An improv audience prefers watching the action.

All of this is a part of taking the active choice — show the audience, don't tell them.

SILENCE IS GOLDEN

Too many performers are terrified when the stage is quiet, but a few moments of silence doesn't mean nothing is happening. Just the opposite — it often leads into the most important moments in a scene.

An improviser needs to consider the most intelligent response he can give to a statement, and so he must feel he can take the time to stop and think. These moments of silence make a beginning improviser very nervous. He often tries to fill the silence with useless chatter, which only adds clutter to the scene.

Improvisers have no reason to fear silence — in fact, more experienced players learn to appreciate it. The silence creates tension and draws in the audience. There is action in thought, and the audience finds a player's response worth waiting for.

When an actor has a strong initiation, but becomes very verbose, he diminishes the importance of the line, and babbles away the energy behind his ideas.

By taking his time and being thoughtful about his work, a player ends up economizing his words; he discovers that he can say more by saying less. The actor's cliché is very true: less *is* more.

THE RULE OF THREES

For some inexplicable reason, things are funnier when they happen three times. Two isn't enough, and four is too many, but the third time something happens, it usually gets a laugh. This is a basic, but mysterious, rule of comedy. The same mechanism in the brain that likes to see patterns seems to thrive on this "Rule of Threes."

Del teaches pattern recognition in workshops, not to train actors to do it, but to demonstrate that all human beings *already have* an extremely sophisticated pattern mechanism in their heads.

"They needn't worry about things like structure — it's already there," he says. "The 'Rule of Threes' is a deeply ingrained biological phenomenon. "Nobody really knows why it's funnier when things happen three times, but I have a theory. We have three brains — the neo-cortex, the mammalian cortex, and the reptilian cortex. My theory is that each brain gets a joke at a different rate. Of course, it might be something else entirely!"

KEY POINTS FOR CHAPTER SEVEN

*Keep it simple. Less is more.

*Avoid exposition.

*Start scenes in the middle.

*Take the active choice to forward action.

*Be specific. Avoid generalities.

*Listen for the game move.

*Welcome the silences. There is action in thought.

CHAPTER EIGHT
One Mind, Many Bodies

Following the Unconscious Choice

The subconscious is a lot smarter than most people think.

Very often, when a beginning improviser gets the impulse to say or do something in a scene, he ignores it.

When his subconscious provides him with a sudden idea for the scene, and he doesn't understand the reason for making this "crazy" choice, his ego considers it a mistake. The only *real* mistake here is ignoring the inner voice.

Inexperienced players disregard the unconscious choice, and continue on with the scene as if that choice was never made; it doesn't fit in with what they "think" the scene is about.

They couldn't be more wrong. As explained in the previous chapters, a scene is *never* about what the player thinks it is going to be; glossing over this "mistake" actually ruins a great chance to make discoveries.

As the players grow more experienced on stage, they discover they have an inner voice which, when followed, leads them to interesting twists in the scene. The unusual choices result in the most interesting scenes.

The ego is the part of the mind that hangs on to preconceived notions about scenes, so the best improvisers always strive to overcome their own egos. They've learned to trust their inner voices to their unconscious right choices.

And when a player reaches the level where he lets his subconscious make the correct choices, his level of confidence on stage will soar! One of the most difficult feats for a beginning improviser is trusting his unconscious mind to lead him down the right path. Eventually, he learns that there is a part of his brain that really does know how to do this work quite well — if he would just get out of his own way!

THE GROUP MIND

After an improviser learns to trust and follow his own inner voice, he begins to do the same with his fellow players' inner voices. Once he puts his own ego out of the way, he stops judging the ideas of others — instead, he considers them brilliant, and eagerly follows them!

This is why there is no such thing as a "bad idea" in improv. Players take each other's ideas — no matter what they are — and make them work. As we know, the actor's business is to justify. One person's idea becomes the collective idea of the group, and is therefore played brilliantly.

In the world outside of improv, the more minds that are involved in an undertaking, the lower the intelligence of the group — just look at the government (any government), or most TV and films that are created by committee! Too many cooks definitely spoil the broth.

The situation is very different with improvisation. We already know that people have incredible individual capabilities. Unlike the real world, however, when a number of players are on stage, their intelligence is actually *increased*. The group intelligence is much more than the sum of its parts.

When a team of improvisers pays close attention to each other, hearing and remembering everything, and respecting all that they hear, a group mind forms. The goal of this phenomenon is to connect the information created out of group ideas — and it's easily capable of brilliance.

People who have never experienced it may be skeptical, dismissing it as New Age nonsense, but the group mind is a very real phenomenon. This is not to say that each person can read the others' minds or project specific thoughts; but when a group mind is achieved, its members have a very strong sense of the group as an entity of its own, and connects with its feelings and requirements. There is an empathy among the individuals involved, almost an instinct. The members exist to serve the needs of the group, much like the Innuit Indians who place themselves in a group trance to attack a polar bear or a whale. If everyone fails to do the right thing, they will die!

This "group mind" is not a phenomenon exclusive to insects and improvisers, though. As cited in the previous chapter, a football team is at its best when everyone knows what everyone else is doing, and other groups working closely toward a common goal may also achieve this state. Still, it is very difficult to describe, and not always achieved.

Many improvisers experience that feeling of amazement that comes from leaving the stage, saying to their fellow players, "How the hell did we *do* that?!" When they break it down and try to analyze it, they discover that the Harold is simply created by the group process — following each moment, step by step, never forgetting anything. They always accept the ideas of the other players without judging them to be "good" or "bad," always thinking, "This is now *our* idea."

The ImprovOlympic workshops constantly prove that a group can achieve powers greater than the individual human mind. Scenes created have turned out to be prophetic, and ESP has actually occurred on stage. Players are able to speak simultaneously, at a normal rate of speed, saying the exact same thing, word for word. Some teams became oracles on stage, answering the great questions of the universe, one word at a time, leaving audiences chilled and astonished.

Audiences have witnessed the group mind linking up to a universal intelligence, enabling them to perform fantastic, sometimes unbelievable feats. It only happens when the group members are finely attuned to each other, but it almost seems like they are tapping into the same universal consciousness that enables individuals with special abilities. Somehow, we are able to connect to it — and all improvisers know the value of connections!

THE COCKTAIL PARTY

The Cocktail Party is an exercise that allows the actors to experience the process of the group mind, and makes an excellent opening game in a Harold. It also teaches players to give and take focus in group scenes, as well as allowing players to discover levels of meaning and connections within their work.

At one time, large group scenes were considered dangerous and difficult to pull off. There is no reason why a large group of people should have trouble on stage, as long as everyone knows where the *focus* of the scene is. Of course, the focus can be — and usually is — passed around the stage just as a volleyball is batted around a court.

One of the best ways to teach the give and take of focus is the Cocktail Party game.

The group is broken up into pairs, and told they are couples at a cocktail party. They are scattered around the stage, so there is some space between each couple. Each pair is given a number, and when it is called out by an outside director, that couple and their conversation takes focus.

Each couple is involved in a separate conversation when their number is called, and when another number is called, the focus is passed to the next couple. All the other couples quietly listen to the couple who has the focus, although they behave as if they are still involved in conversation with their partners. Each time a number is called, the last couple speaking gives up the focus to the next couple.

After one round of discussions, numbers are no longer called out. The players must pass the focus by themselves. The actors must edit each other every time a thought has been completed by a couple.

Very quickly, a natural rhythm develops, and the actors pass the focus more and more rapidly. They can sense when the person speaking is ready to pass the focus, and they learn that focus can be given, as well as taken.

At the beginning of the game, the couples' topics of discussion are as different from each other as possible. This chaos is necessary, so that the group mind can utilize it in interesting ways. No matter how different the topics are kept at the beginning, they always connect by the end of the game, usually in the most unexpected ways.

The discussion topics are like the poles of a teepee. At the bottom, the poles are far apart, but as they progress upward, they get closer together, until they finally connect at the top. This principle is often utilized in a Harold as well — the farther apart the scenes or discussion topics, the more amazing it is when they finally all connect.

Since each individual in the Cocktail Party game can hear everything that is being said, the group mind can commence its takeover. The separate conversations begin to connect on various levels, and individual ideas are unified into a much larger theme. This is all accomplished as a result of the group mind.

The following example of a Cocktail Party game was performed by four pairs of improvisers.

One of the persons in Couple # 1 is discussing his teaching job, and how he is affected by the banning of books.

Couple #2 is discussing political dealings between the Russian republics and the U.S. president.

Couple #3 is commenting on the rescue of trapped whales in the Arctic.

And Couple #4 is talking about mass murderers.

Here are how the conversations advanced:

COUPLE 1: "Book banning in schools is done out of ignorance."
"I agree. Children need to learn about their world. Their learning shouldn't be censored."

COUPLE 3: "I was happy that people cared to save those whales that were stuck in the ice."
"It's nice that man has befriended a species for a change, instead of killing it."

COUPLE 4: "I read a book about mass murderers. It said they believe they are inevitable products of society."

COUPLE 2: "Glasnost was an important step."
"It's nice to see better relations with the Russians."

COUPLE 3: "It's like a fairy tale come true. Russia and the U.S. coming together to break the ice and free the whales."

COUPLE 1: "I can't teach *Huckleberry Finn*. It's a classic. So now, I have my class reading *Moby Dick*. They don't like it very much."
"Why not?"
"They don't like the idea of wanting revenge on a whale."

COUPLE 4: "Some kill because they want revenge on people they hate."
"Insane."

"Actually, some are thought to be sane."

COUPLE 3: "If we could only stop killing whales and dolphins. They're so intelligent."
"Unfortunately, *we* aren't. We save them, but we kill them."
"It's sick."

COUPLE 1: "Is Ahab too much of a fanatic for your students?"
"No, it's not that. They want gore . . . like the senseless violence they get from *Friday the 13th.*"

COUPLE 4: "It's hard to follow the logic of someone that crazy."

COUPLE 2: "Just think: peace throughout the world. Now *that's* a fairy tale."

COUPLE 4: "Society is changing and our criminals are approaching the norm."

COUPLE 3: "It's criminal. The world is for us, yet we destroy it."

COUPLE 2: "Maybe the next generation will save the world."

COUPLE 1: "This new generation was raised on senseless violence."

COUPLE 3: "I'm all for saving the whales. Let's pray we can save ourselves."

The conversations all progress and heighten, but the sections of each couples' dialog become shorter and shorter as the piece grows. We can see a major theme emerge out of the conversations, one that could not be planned ahead of time. This theme could be explored further, if the Cocktail Party were used as an opening for a Harold. In the case of this example, the Harold would focus on the next generation and their responsibilities to the world they have inherited.

REFLECTION SCENES

This exercise is a series of two-person scenes that reflect the ideas of the entire group.

It begins with two actors starting a scene without any input on the themes or locations. They must complete a scene that is as rich as possible, both physically and verbally. When this scene is completed, another two players take the stage. They improvise a totally different scene, but one that somehow is inspired by something they noticed in the previous scene. It can be a physical inspiration, or an idea created by the theme developed out of the previous scene. It can be anything at all, as long as there is something derived from the first scene.

A third scene is then improvised by two players who are inspired by anything they saw in the previous two scenes, and so on.

This example of a reflection exercise took place in a workshop situation.

Scene one involved a young woman and her domineering parents. The woman was tired of feeling inferior, so she decided to join the army and "be all that she could be."

The second scene revealed a relationship between two roommates who had been friends since childhood, a friendship threatened when one of them turned "punk." His new clothes, earrings, and shaved haircut would be unacceptable at the places the two of them used to visit together. To solve the problem of not being able to go out together, the punk roommate transformed his conservative roommate to a punk look that can be used on a temporary basis.

Scene three took place at a car dealership, where a man wanted to buy a Porsche. The salesman thought the customer looked too conservative to drive such a flashy car, and wanting a satisfied customer, tried selling him a car more suitable to his image.

The fourth scene was at a carnival, where two workers

were observing people from the big city, noting the differences ranging from punkers to yuppies. But no matter what the customers looked like, the carnies put them all into one category — "marks."

Scene five portrayed a man attempting his first parachute jump. We learned he was in training for the Air Force, and that this jump was one of the many tests he was facing to overcome his fears. As the plane increased its altitude, he noticed a carnival below in the distance.

These scenes all seemed to reflect attitudes about self-image, and the image that others perceive. The scenes also connected on a physical level. The punkers seen at the carnival were obviously the roommates from the second scene, and the carnival itself was the same one seen from the plane by the reluctant paratrooper. The Air Force scene was inspired by the line from the first scene, "Be all that you can be."

If this piece had been an actual Harold, the Air Force trainee would have undoubtedly met the young woman from the first scene, after she had joined the service.

When doing reflection scenes, the group begins to notice ideas that are constantly being recycled on many levels. Soon, these totally separate scenes each become a part of a large group piece, from which a major theme emerges.

Another example of a series of reflection scenes began with a Tai Chi class between a master and his student. The spiritually heightened master teaches his student how to join him on the spiritual plane; the scene also has sexual overtones, as both are orgasmic when they reach the same spiritual plane.

The second scene saw an Eastern Indian cab driver pick up a fare who turns out to be a New Age crystal salesman. The salesman has a crystal for every ailment, including one for masculinity and fertility, which seems to be the cab driver's problem.

Scene three was a meeting for singles called the "I'm Sensational Club." A man approaches a woman saying, "You're sensational," the mandatory greeting for the club. She comments on his huge "aura," another sexual overtone. They compare their astrology signs and spirituality, and can't believe how perfect they are for each other. They discuss being drawn together spiritually from across the room. At the end of the scene, they are the only two members who show up for the meeting.

In the fourth scene, a man adrift in his broken down speedboat is approached by another man in a kayak. The man in the kayak offers to help the stranded man, and while preparing to tow the speedboat, the man in the kayak discusses his oneness with nature. Holding a rope in his teeth, he tows the speedboat as he rows the kayak. The man sitting in the speedboat being towed shouts, "You're sensational!"

As a group, the ideas reflected spirituality and sexuality for the New Age movement.

The different sides of a diamond all reflect each other. Harold players should do the same thing — reflect each other's ideas.

KEY POINTS FOR CHAPTER EIGHT
*Take the unusual choice.
*Listen to your inner voice.
*Reflect each other's ideas.

CHAPTER NINE
Environmentally Aware

All human beings have a sense memory that can summon up a past sound, sight, or smell. The sound of a dentist's drill or the smell of freshly cut grass immediately conjures up precise memories of past experiences. When improvisers learn to recall such clues, they can turn them to their own advantage on stage.

It is simple to cause such a re-creation in one's mind, because everything perceived comes from inside the head. Once the improviser learns to trigger that visual creation in his own brain, he begins to create that environment for his audience.

Most of us have experienced this phenomenon ourselves. Charna was recently sitting in a club where some groups were performing, when she noticed a sign hanging on one of the stage flats across the room. She was too far away to make out the words, so after a few minutes of squinting, she asked one of the directors what was on the sign. He said, "It says, 'AUSTRALIA OR BUST.'"

"Suddenly, to my astonishment, I was able to make out the words perfectly," she says. "The same sign that, just a few seconds earlier, was too far away for my eyes to read, could now be seen clearly. Every letter!"

A similar experience is common with sound. Many of us have heard a popular song several times, but can't make out the lyrics. After we learn the actual words, they seem very obvious, and we can't imagine how we *couldn't* have understood them!

Anyone can re-create a visual revelation for himself by asking a friend to hold up a newspaper with a headline. If he stands just far enough away so that the words cannot be made out and asks the friend with the newspaper to tell him what the headline says, he will discover that he can suddenly read it himself!

How can this be? If the sight lines were too distant for his eyes to pick up, why can he see it now?

Everything that we perceive is truly perceived inside the head. As soon as an actor begins to *see* his environment on stage, the audience sees it through his eyes. The environment affects him and the choices he makes in the scene. A scene set at a circus will be very different than that same scene set inside a cathedral.

The following scene was improvised in a workshop exploring the effects of the environment. Two students were told they must create a scene that takes place on a deserted highway. Both men, Tom and Roger, looked around in silence and seemed dazed. Standing far apart from each other and showing vast amounts of space, each seemed lost, lonely and worried:

TOM: I have a theory why we haven't seen people for days. I think there was a nuclear exchange, and somehow we were the only ones who weren't killed.

ROGER: I'll buy that. Even the last town we walked through was deserted.

TOM: Well, I guess we have to start over. We need a president.

ROGER: Okay.

TOM: I nominate myself.

ROGER: I second that.

TOM: Does that mean I'm president?

ROGER: No, it just means you're nominated. We have to have an election.

(They vote, and Roger counts the secret ballots.)

ROGER: You lost. I don't know how, either, because I voted for you.

TOM: Then I declare a dictatorship. But, I appoint you attorney general.

ROGER: Great! Then I get to prosecute someone.

(Looks around.) Well, since you're the only one here, I guess I'll prosecute you for the state of the world.

TOM: Okay.

ROGER: I find you guilty.

TOM: But you haven't proven anything yet.

ROGER: This is a dictatorship! There's no due process of law.

TOM: I'm defecting.

As the scene continued, there was a summit in the middle of the highway to discuss trade negotiations. The pair began fighting, and the threat of war was once again at hand. The two players were clearly affected by the desolate environment they had visualized in their heads.

Improvisers must totally commit to their environment, because as easily as they create a location for their audience, they can destroy it. It is very jarring to see an elaborate environment created on stage, in which everybody knows where every imaginary object is on stage, only to see an actor walk through a table and destroy everything the players worked so hard to establish.

This is one of the most common forms of "breaking reality," one of the worst mistakes an improviser can make; this is discussed in detail in the next chapter.

Players who commit to the environment respect all objects created on stage as though they were real, because once the performers bring them into existence, they *are* real. If players don't commit to them 100 per cent, they will not commit to anything.

Any audience that has watched enough inexperienced improvisers has seen some truly astonishing things, feats to challenge a Houdini. Drinking glasses vanish and re-appear, telephones magically grow and shrink several times in a few seconds, and people walk through tables, chairs, and walls.

Performers who do this are obviously not visualizing their environment.

Most audiences stop paying attention to a scene like this, and instead concentrate on the many ways the player has destroyed his reality. This is a form of denial, and it can only be avoided if each player pays close attention to the physical details created by *everyone* on stage.

An environment created on stage nearly always has a six-sided "where." In other words, there is something in front of, behind, on either side of, above and below the players. There are truly an unlimited number of objects that cause the improviser to feel a certain way. Many people believe "You are what you eat," but in theatre, "You are what you do."

The objects created on stage influence the actors' choices, and help to discover emotions and attitudes. As soon as a player begins an activity, his mind discovers why, and he justifies it in his attitude.

If a woman is discussing the blind date she had the night before, she may not have a clue as to how she feels. But, if she is preparing a salad as she discusses the date, the motion of tearing apart the head of lettuce may put her in a violent state. The anger she feels about the blind date is put across subtly through her activity as she discusses the disastrous evening. This brings her information to a visual, as well as a verbal level. In fact, she can strengthen the effect if she verbally plays down her anger, while she is violently tearing the lettuce to shreds.

This player discovered her emotional state through the activity in her environment. Why is she making salad in the first place? Maybe her date insulted her figure, and she has discovered she is concerned about her weight problem.

Objects in a scene are there to help lead a player who feels stuck. They should prompt the improviser to *discover*, rather than *invent*.

One example, a scene that took place in a store, shows how

an object in the environment led directly to the discovery of that scene.

Anna was searching through imaginary toys, picking up each one and then setting it down again. She was finally directed to choose just *one* toy and let that inspire her, to give her information as to why she was there and what was on her mind. She picked up the object, which became a doll. She slowly brought it to her chest, hugged it, and began to cry. Her husband in the scene immediately rushed to her side to comfort her. It was a touching moment, leading to a wonderful scene about a couple who lost a child, and thought they couldn't have any more children. Although the scene later took many twists, the initial discovery came from a simple object in the environment.

Visualizing objects in an environment always rescues a player who becomes temporarily stuck in a scene. One example started as a scene between a father and a son:

FATHER: I am very angry.

SON: I know, Dad, I came to apologize.

At this point, the first player became momentarily stuck. So, he utilized his training, and looked around his environment to help him along. He picked up a newspaper and looked at it, which led to his next line:

FATHER: It's in all the papers. The whole town knows.

The simple discovery of the newspaper raised the stakes in the scene, and gave the players a better idea of the seriousness of the son's situation.

When making choices, specifics are *always* better than generalities. Specifics add dimensions to the work and to the characters. If an actor offers someone a ride in his Z-28, it gives us more information about his character than if he has just offered a ride in his "car." Just knowing whether a player drives a Yugo, a Studebaker, a Ford pickup truck, or a BMW tells us a great deal about his character.

Truth in Comedy

Mike Myers of *Saturday Night Live* and *Wayne's World* fame was especially meticulous about this rule. Even in his scenes at the ImprovOlympic and Second City, he was specific. In a dinner scene, he'd never say, "Pass the ketchup." It would only be, "Pass the Heinz."

During a class Mike was teaching at the ImprovOlympic, he created a non-specific character that he called "Vague-Man" to emphasize the point to students.

"I'm Vague-Man! I *work!*"

Where?

"At *the store!* I do *things!* I've got to go *someplace* now! I'm Vague-Man!"

The more specific the choices, the easier they connect to future scenes, and players should always be aware of connections. Characters in a future scene may pass a stalled car by the side of the road; if that stalled car is a Z-28, then a connection is made. (Hemingway knew the value of specific information. That's why, in *The Killers*, a character doesn't just eat a candy bar — he munches a Baby Ruth.)

Of course, while an environment and the objects within it affect the scene, they should not *be* the scene. Many beginning improvisers make the mistake of discussing the activity they are engaged in, which is redundant when the activity is being done properly. Paradoxically, the scene is usually the most effective if the conversation is as far removed from the activity as possible.

There are several improv games that teach this, including one requiring players to perform one activity while discussing another topic (audience suggestions supply the activity and the topic). One memorable scene was performed by the team Friends of the Zoo — they were to perform surgery while discussing restaurants. They were able to brilliantly reflect both suggestions; while one player talked about barbecued ribs, the group was obviously sawing away at the patient's chest, and so on.

Experienced performers learn that their dialog isn't about their activity. Instead, the lines should be saved for the *relationship* with the other player. That relationship is created while the players are engaged in their particular activity.

However, if all they discuss is the activity itself, there's no chance for a scene — they might as well save their breath. The blind date scene was not about making a salad — it was about rejection by men. The verbal and visual levels of a scene must be kept separate, so they can connect *later*.

One exercise that encourages beginning performers to explore their environment involves the use of objects.

CREATE AN OBJECT, SAY A LINE

This is a simple exercise, in which two players begin a scene. Before each of them speaks a line of dialog, however, they must create and use an object. This is done every time a player delivers a line — he cannot keep using the same object over and over again. In this way, he continues to make discoveries throughout the scene.

Of course, the objects are not there to be discussed ("I'm going to fill this glass full of water. Now I'm going to drink it."). What is clearly *seen* does not need to be *heard*.

Both players soon discover their attitudes through their activities and objects. Before they know it, they won't be concentrating on creating objects — they'll be too busy following their scene! The objects automatically pop up right and left.

This is also an excellent exercise for beginning players, because it slows them down and forces them to think about what is said to them. Since they must take the time to create an object before they respond, they must also use those extra moments to consider the meaning behind their partner's speech. This requirement may annoy some actors, and they have to be reminded how helpful this exercise is to their scenes!

Usually, we are stricter about following rules at the beginning of scenes, but once they are underway, the physical and verbal level flow naturally.

Following is an example of a scene that came from the "Create an Object to Speak" exercise:

[WOMAN #1 rolls in a wheelbarrow (and is therefore allowed to speak her first line).]

WOMAN #1:   On the way home, I saw a woman getting mugged.

[WOMAN #2 tears open a big bag and pours it into the wheelbarrow (and can now speak her line).]

WOMAN #2:   While I was riding the El train today, I saw a man pull a gold chain off someone's neck.

[WOMAN #1 stirs the contents of the wheelbarrow with a stick, and can say her second line.]

WOMAN #1:   It's not safe to walk the streets anymore.

[WOMAN #2 picks up a trowel and bricks, and scoops what is now discovered to be cement from the wheelbarrow, and speaks again while she lays a brick.]

WOMAN #2:   I never go out without my mace or stun gun.

Now both women are ensconced in their activity, discussing crime in the neighborhood while building a brick wall in front of them. With their last line, "Nobody's going to get us," they discover they have built a wall around themselves, isolating them from the outside world. Here, the physical level of the scene successfully connected with the verbal level, making a wonderful scene about an attempt to stay safe in today's violent world.

VISUAL GROUP CREATION: THE INVOCATION

Del created an exercise where students invoke a "god" that they create themselves from their own group vision. It's not as frightening as it may sound, and it actually involves the "group mind" state discussed in the previous chapter. This god, and his or her characteristics, then influences the scenes which follow.

There are three steps for a group to follow to invoke this god.

Step One: Describe It

One at a time, each student looks ahead into the space where it is to be created, and describes a bit of this god. This vision appears as the students slowly relinquish their individual visions for the group's vision. No one ever denies what has been said — they accept it and see it themselves:

EXAMPLE:

It is green, and it smells bad.

It is laughing and babbling.

It has a big mouth.

It is square, like an ice cube.

It is slimy.

Step Two: Talk Directly to It

By doing this, the group gives the god a lifelike quality, and some other-than-physical characteristics:

EXAMPLE:

You try to control things all the time.

You are always telling jokes.

You are always laughing at your own jokes.

You are the only one who laughs at your jokes.

Step Three: Worship the God

The players raise their creation to a level of power. Speaking in heightened, formal language, slowly and adoringly, usually helps bring this about:

EXAMPLE:

Thou art the king of bad judgment.

Thy voice is no comfort to my ears.

Thou hast taken control of my good sense.

When thou art with me, I am debased and dishonored.

From this particular invocation, the players were inspired in their subsequent scenes, as the images they created were strong and ever-present in their minds and their work.

In one scene, two players were searching for a mysterious spirit in an old house. While searching for clues to the mystery of this entity, they were quickly overwhelmed by a nasty odor. One of the players discovered a locked door and rapped on it saying, "Knock, knock." The other player said, "Who's there?" Suddenly, they were telling bad "knock-knock" jokes. They realized their worst fears had come true — they were under the evil spell of the mysterious spirit of the house.

The following scene saw two stand-up comics backstage at a concert, discussing the previous show. Although one of them had received a standing ovation, the other one had not connected at all because his material was so bad. Reality was trying to tell him to give up his comedy career, and he tried to face the fact that he was a bad stand-up.

Unknowingly, the group managed to invoke the archetypal "bad comedian," and elevate it to a god! The work was driven by the demon that sometimes gets in the way of our brilliant scenes by forcing us to go for bad jokes — a slimy, smelly creature with bad taste!

A second group invoked a blob with eight legs, a bad toupee, and a cigar in its mouth; it was covered with chocolate. It became clear that this was the archetypal talent agent. One scene saw the agent on four different phones, making deals, lying, and sweet-talking his way out of things, while sugar-coating everything he said.

The images created by the group mind were clearly hanging in the air, and very definitely affected the scenes on stage which followed. While the group invoked an archetype which had power over their work, the power truly came from them.

Visual group creation is the most vital part of the invocation. This is certainly not limited to the creation of a "god." Human qualities like greed or virtue can be used. If a team invokes a quality and raises it to the level of archetype, then they can become it and be affected by it, rather than just discuss it.

Some of the most successful invocations also involve mundane, everyday objects that are raised to high status, objects like a pencil or a comb. The team must imagine the object in front of them, and enlarge it to a thousand times its normal size in their mind. They will be amazed at the details they can see, and the types of ideas that grow out of the invocation. The process is the same: *describe it, talk to it, worship it.* Sometimes a fourth step, *become it,* is added. The Invocation Game is a wonderful opening for a Harold, as it can inspire so many scenes and characters from a simple audience suggestion!

When invoking a human quality, abstract qualities are projected onto the group creation in the form of physical details. When invoking an object, the visual details inspire human traits, emotional responses, memories and character quirks.

If the pencil were invoked, for example, a wealth of information could be gleaned from physical details. Teeth marks might inspire a nervous character. An eraser that wears down more rapidly than the point could suggest someone who makes a lot of mistakes, or a perfectionist who is never satisfied. The "Number Two" label might conjure up memories of standardized testing, while "red" could suggest anything from debts to spelling errors. All from a simple pencil!

Following is an example of the invocation of a cigarette:
DESCRIBE IT:
> It is white with a long green line. Its filter is white, and it has three separate chambers. It says "Virginia Slims."

TALK TO IT:
> You've come a long way, baby.

You make me bold.

You make my teeth yellow.

You make me cough. I hate you, but I need you.

You keep me calm.

WORSHIP IT:

Thou hast the power to control my nervous system.

Thou art a thing of nature.

Thou canst snuff out my life with thy smoke.

I am addicted to thee.

Thou chokest me and I return for thee.

BECOME IT:

I am the cigarette that you always seek.

How dare you crush me under your feet.

I will have the last laugh.

I will get you through that big exam you must take.

Calm down. I will be with you forever!

This invocation inspired scenes about feminism (Virginia Slims), a controlling person, and someone who made her friends sick whenever she entered a room.

Probably the most powerful invocation in improv history occurred with the Second City cast in Toronto a few years ago, according to Mike Myers. The company was having trouble with a scene, and they wondered what Del Close would do. Mike decided to have the cast invoke Del for his advice, an exercise he had experienced in ImprovOlympic workshops. The cast proceeded to invoke Del. As they reached their peak, suddenly Del himself stepped out of the darkness in the back of the theatre!

"The cast freaked out! Everybody screamed," laughs Myers. None of them knew that Del had flown into Canada on business that week, and just happened to stop by the theatre when the company was performing the invocation.

CHARACTER MOTIVATION

Wear your character like a straw boater.
— *Paul Sills*

Many potentially wonderful scenes come to a dead halt because the actor is concerned about what his "character" is doing or saying in a specific situation.

It is impossible for the *character* an actor is playing to get stuck. It isn't the character who is stuck, but the actor himself. Since this "character" shares his mind, his intelligence, and his morals, the player must reveal *himself* in this person.

When improvisers realize that all they need to do is react honestly, their scenes come alive with real human relationships. They interact in social situations that everyone relates to.

Too many would-be improvisers think using a funny voice or wearing a silly costume is all that is needed in playing a character. These are actually only incidental embellishments. A real character consists of the actor himself, with any additional point of view, preoccupation, or attitude that this character has. This additional point of view motivates his responses in specific ways.

One exercise called Secrets is used in workshops to show how a preoccupation adds a dimension to a character.

SECRETS

Each player is given a piece of paper with a great secret or desire written on it (the suggestions may be written previously by the group). Some of these may include:

"I'm psychic."
"I'm desperate to make a friend."
"I'm going to commit suicide."
"I'm illiterate, and scared others will find out."
"I always fall in love at first sight."

Two players each pick their own secret, which is revealed to the audience, but not to each other. The players are then given a location which is, of course, unrelated to any of the preoccupations. As always, the players create a scene, but with their secrets in mind. They discover that their responses are motivated by their characters' preoccupations. Those responses are therefore different than usual, and the players discover how they are affected by these new attitudes.

WARNING! This is not a guessing game! Players should not try to discover each other's secrets — only be affected by their own. If the players reveal their "subtext" (although strictly speaking, there is no "text" in improvisation), they cheapen it and render it impotent. Having these secrets in mind gives the players the most subtle responses on unrelated matters.

It is interesting to see how these separate preoccupations combine to create an exciting dynamic in a scene. An intuitive actor easily sees the preoccupation of his fellow actor and plays right into his hands. Although this isn't the purpose of the game, it is always interesting to watch.

One example of this exercise was performed by Jim Carrane, who had the secret, "I'm planning to commit suicide."

His scene was set in a bowling alley. Without mentioning his plan, he internalized it in everything he said and did. He knew he was a lousy bowler, and carelessly threw the ball without aiming. Solemnly, he would say, "It's just a game. Who cares?" When keeping score, he wrote much more than just a number — indicating that he was scribbling bits and pieces of his suicide note. After adding up the final scores of the game, again writing more than necessary, he asked his date if he could borrow her car for a couple of hours. Throughout the scene, however, he never mentioned his motives, even though he was completely driven by them.

Every director has heard the dreaded, familiar "My character wouldn't do that." There is *nothing* a *character* won't do. When an actor discovers a new character in his personality, he must find what will make him go further — to do the unexpected. Developing characters proved to be one of the most useful elements of the Harold for Chris Farley when he moved on to *Saturday Night Live*.

"I was able to come up with many different characters. In one Harold, I could do five characters, and maybe hone those just a little bit and try 'em again," says Farley. "There are so many different characters you can do in one given Harold — five characters can easily emerge."

KEY POINTS FOR CHAPTER NINE
*Commit to the physical.
*Let your environment affect you.
*Be specific with your objects.
*Reveal yourself through your character.

CHAPTER TEN
Responsibilities of a Harold Player

An actor has more responsibility in improvisation than any other theatre form.

In a movie or a play, the performer must follow the orders of his director and give the best performance possible. As long as he remembers his lines and delivers them as well as he is able, he holds up his part of the production and does his job.

With improv, however, the actor is responsible for nearly everything. There is no one else to plan sets, props or sound effects. Although he is trained by a director, once the actor steps on stage, he is editor, choreographer, composer, singer, dancer, writer, director and improviser.

This is quite a bit of responsibility for an actor, but fortunately, he is not the only one with those jobs.

He is part of a team.

HOW TO BE A GOOD TEAM PLAYER

The Harold is just like football, baseball, or any other team sport — no one player is more important than anyone else.

Each player must share the responsibility. On an eight-man team, each player should do one-eighth of the work. If one person tries to lead a Harold, it is doomed to fail — the Harold must be followed by the group.

The best Harold player thinks of himself as a tool for the Harold, and tries to find his function in the piece, sublimating himself to the needs of the work. He is always thinking of the Harold, and what is needed throughout every moment of the game. He should not be thinking of himself. In fact, it is just as important for the player to know when he is *not* needed on stage. He should always believe that "seeing Harold" is more important than being seen by friends and family in the audience.

Many times, the best Harold players will do very little in an improvisation simply because they do not see a part for themselves. When the major tasks are taken care of by other team players, they are naturally there to provide support and back-up for whatever ensemble work is required. Although they are standing by and ready if needed, they do not get in the way of the game if they are not.

Bill Murray understands the importance of listening to others when improvising. According to Del, Bill's willingness to listen made him invaluable whenever he played a supporting role during a scene, although he was equally adept at taking the lead (his ability to listen was partly developed, according to his brother Joel, while growing up in a large family and trying to hold his own during conversations at the dinner table).

Like all the best improvisers, Bill Murray is as talented supporting others during an improv as he is at leading scenes. While working with a group of professional actors during a week studying with the ImprovOlympic, Bill was performing on a seven-person team one afternoon. Instead of directly involving himself in the first three two-person scenes, he stood back and let them develop. It wasn't until a scene moved to a high school prom that Bill suddenly grabbed a partner and started slow-dancing in the background while the scene progressed downstage (naturally, another pair of dancers immediately joined the background to provide more support and atmosphere).

Few ImprovOlympic performers have been better at support than Chris Farley of *Saturday Night Live*. He is able to grab one line and make a meal out of it, as he did in his role as a security guard in *Wayne's World*. Del says Chris can get more out of one line than anybody he's ever known. "I have to," jokes Chris about his *SNL* work. "That's all they write for me!"

Mike Myers is also an excellent ensemble player; while working with the ImprovOlympic, he was always adding color to other people's scenes. When somebody got an idea, Mike would be the light bulb above their heads; when someone was stabbed, Mike provided the spurting blood.

The best Harold players know that it is much more satisfying to have a small part in creating a great Harold, than sacrificing the Harold so they can be seen.

Unfortunately, some bright, funny players aren't able to keep their egos in check. They enter a scene and lead it in a direction that suits their ideas, rather than follow it in the direction it is heading. They try to control the Harold — as if they could be the star without destroying the Harold! If one person controls the Harold, it is no longer a *group* effort, and the *group mind* is destroyed.

As intelligent as some of these players are, they can't (or won't) trust in the concept of team players — as a result, no one trusts them. Such players discover that no one is willing to play with them, because they consider themselves more important than the game.

When an improviser goes on stage to play Harold, he must be willing to be a saint for the duration of the performance. Their off-stage lives may be radically different, but on stage, the best players must strive for sainthood!

THE PLAYER AS EDITOR

To edit a scene, a player walks onto the center of the stage and initiates the next scene or game. He simply waits for the right moment, then crosses in front of the existing scene, thus beginning the next one. The scene being cut slowly fades back upstage, where the remaining Harold players are waiting and watching for their roles to become apparent.

Learning how to edit a scene is easy. Knowing *when* to cut a scene off requires a little more effort.

Players have to respect the length and timing of the individual pieces that make up the Harold. If a scene or a game goes on for too long, not only does it detract from that piece, it zaps the energy of the entire performance. A Harold should rarely run longer than 35 minutes. Since the opening alone can take six or seven minutes, the entire Harold becomes unbalanced if one scene rambles on without being cut off by other players.

By using a cinematic approach, the player is responsible for seeing that his fellow players are edited at the right time. This is really very easy to do, since most of us have seen thousands of hours of TV and movies — it's almost instinctual! Based on how much film and TV we've seen, most of us have the equivalent of advanced degrees in film editing.

Any player paying attention knows when his teammates have established their relationship in a scene clearly enough to be cut until a future time. It will be obvious when a scene reaches its end, and the players will need to be cut so that they can retire their brains. When improvisers work together for a while, they will recognize the tone in another player's voice asking to be edited.

Much of this is pure instinct. If a player has an impulse to cut a scene but isn't quite sure if the timing is right, chances are that his impulse was the correct one. He can't worry about being polite — it's more polite to edit a scene too soon than too late, because they can always return with their ideas later. That's the beauty of Harold!

THE PLAYER AS DIRECTOR

When a player edits a scene, this means he's decided it's time for another scene, or perhaps a game or monolog. The ball is in his court, until the next editor/director deems it necessary to take over.

As a director, a player may choose to enter a scene, rather than cut it off. "Walk-ons" are appropriate if a performer has an idea to help move the scene forward in the same direction that its players are moving it. Often, actors in a scene call for another player to enter, so the team members should always be listening for that call.

Good walk-ons enter, give their initiation, and then exit. A walk-on must remember that the scene is not about him; he shouldn't re-direct the scene or become its focus. And he shouldn't enter in the first place if he doesn't have an idea to help the actors move their scene forward, because he only causes further confusion. Don't throw an anchor to a sinking ship — someone else will help. *Don't fix it if it isn't broken!* Players should never invade each other's scenes if they are going smoothly and don't call for assistance.

As a director, a player may even initiate an idea for a split scene that enriches or illuminates the scene currently being performed. To do this, a player begins the split scene on the other side of the stage, instead of walking in front of the ongoing action and cutting it off. By beginning the new scene *next to* the old one, instead of crossing *in front* of it, the other players realize they are about to see a split scene. If there's any confusion, an actor can simply call out "Split scene!"

In such a split scene, two separate scenes continue at the same time, sharing the focus as discussed in previous chapters. As the focus passes back and forth, the two affect each other through the course of the action, while not physically connecting.

A new team learns the proper traffic patterns in order to operate efficiently. Among the most important are *entering* scenes from the rear; *editing* scenes from the front, and initiating *split scenes* from the side.

Betty Thomas (of *Hill Street Blues*) took a chance once at Second City under Del's direction during a three-way split scene. She simply stood up in the middle of her scene and announced, "I'm tired of being in this scene. I want to be in that one over there," and as she walked over and joined the scene on the opposite side of the stage, no one batted an eye. If everyone suddenly started to move to different scenes, the results would have been chaos, but the performers all had the cool to realize that the technique had to be used very sparingly to be effective.

THE PLAYER AS SCENERY

Teamwork can create wonders. Improv groups can turn into just about anything, from animals to rainstorms to trees with serpents slithering through them. During a very patriotic Harold, when the actors in the scene began to sing the national anthem, one of the players standing in the background leaned sideways, and gracefully waved his arms as he became an American flag. The Baron's Barracudas displayed some amazing teamwork when seven players became a trundle bed for the eighth member of their team. In a horizontal line, backs to the audience, the team completed a synchronized backward somersault, landing flat on their backs, ready to be slept on. The move was made in unison without a moment's hesitation, and the audience cheered.

Truth in Comedy

Of course, this is another great thing about improv. Putting up a show is cheap, and yet the scenery and props are unlimited! Since real props cannot be transformed, they become a burden; when actual physical props are sitting around on stage, they limit the improvised creation of other props. Many audience members have difficulty accepting real items on the same stage as imaginary props — and it can be confusing. If there are real props and one invisible prop on stage, the audience sees only the real prop.

And obviously, an invisible table could not hold a real bottle of beer!

THE PLAYER AS SOUND EFFECT

An audience always enjoys watching the back line of players taking care of the performers in a scene. The scene may need sound effects, anything from a police siren to the Voice of God.

If the players in the back line are paying attention, they provide eerie sounds to heighten the mood in a scene, or they may each be pieces of a symphony in a musically orchestrated game.

Of course, too much of a good thing is still too much, and it occasionally reaches that point. If the sound effects become overpowering, they literally become the scene. There is a difference between getting in the way and lending a helping hand.

THE PLAYER AS CHOREOGRAPHER

The actors must always be aware of their movement and blocking in a scene, as well as the "stage picture" they provide in larger group scenes. There's a lot more choreography than that for players to deal with, however.

Many times, a group song or dance arises out of the work. Most improvisers at the ImprovOlympic are not professional singers or dancers, but they always impress audiences with their commitment to doing their best.

Truth in Comedy

Some incredible feats have been achieved through trust. During one Harold the team Grime and Punishment answered the call for a ballet in their Harold. The players attempted to duplicate ballet clichés as they leaped and twirled around the stage, and the audience enjoyed watching Richard Laible lift Mick Napier and twirl him around. The best example of teamwork, was at the climax of the ballet, when, without warning, Mick took a flying leap and hurled himself across the stage, into the arms of his fellow players. There was no doubt in Mick's mind that he would be caught.

These are moments one can only marvel at, yet they occur increasingly often as the trust between team members grows stronger. Players often take enormous leaps of faith, and are seldom betrayed by team members (despite the experience cited in an earlier chapter, which resulted in Del's broken collarbone . . .).

What makes a player literally take a flying leap? Is it merely trust? Is it the raised consciousness of the group? Whatever it is, there is an equivalent feeling that makes the other players get there in time to catch him — one of the most daring examples of improvisational choreography.

CRIMES IN IMPROVISATION

While working on the La Jolla Playhouse production of *The Misanthrope,* director Bob Falls pointed out that a strategy of Cellimone, the female lead, is to keep her suitors off base by asking questions. Her first line is a question: "Is it to subject me to some quick moral quiz/That you have come up here and cornered me like this?"

During their discussion, Falls turned to Del and asked, "What is it about asking questions in improvisation, Del? Isn't that (asking questions) supposed to be the worst thing you can do?"

"You're asking me?" Del responded, to a few muted chuckles. "It's the second worst thing. In improvisation, when you ask a question, you are taking information *away* from your fellow player, instead of *adding* information. It's off-putting. Cuts the ground out from under you."

"*Second* worst thing, eh? What's the worst thing?" asked Falls. Del opened an invisible book under Falls' nose and said, "Here, read this out loud!"

This sort of move is usually called a "pimp," and is not likely to win the performer respect from his fellow players. It is much like asking questions, because it forces a fellow player to *invent* information. Moves which *offer* information allow a fellow player to react and *justify*. Reaction and justification lead to an exciting discovery process *between* the players, which is our goal. Pimping, or asking questions, dumps the burden onto one player, coercing him into dull, forced invention (and probably makes him look bad in the process — another serious improv crime!).

Del speculates that there is a hierarchy of crimes in improvisation, "like an ever-expanding number of infinities." At any rate, there are other candidates for "Worst Crime in Improv," including "reality breaking."

Players break reality when one of them denies the basis of the scene he has helped to create, usually for the sake of a laugh. If one actor shoots another with a space gun during a scene, saying "Pow! Pow!," the other player breaks his reality by saying "Why are you pointing your finger at me and going 'Pow! Pow!'?" To compound the crime, he is also asking a question!

"Reality breaking seldom happens, and is easily trained out of the culprit. One or two severe beatings usually do the job," says Del. "Still, seemingly honest but actually destructive questions pop up all the time, and become part of the improvisational 'clutter' or 'static' that we are so concerned with eliminating."

After players become experienced and understand the reasons for such glaring mistakes, some of them may turn the errors into a game, deliberately violating as many such rules as possible in a short scene.

The earliest example of "breaking reality" that was incorporated into a scene was called "Compass Goofs." According to Del, it was performed by the Compass Players in Chicago around 1956, and was described to him by Severn Darden.

"Two actors established a long dinner table in the center of the stage. They were laying place settings when another actor entered, walked in *through* the invisible dinner table, closed a window directly downstage, walked back through the table and exited," he says.

"Both actors continued with the place settings when a second walk-on entered, walked through their table, and closed the window *again*. He walked back through the table and exited.

"The place setting continued, when a third actor entered, carrying a pail of water, walking through the table, and hurled water through the (twice) closed window. He turned around, discovered the table, and carefully walked around it before exiting."

Reality breaking is extremely rude, even though it can become so outrageously poetic as to become classic. This happened with the original Second City company in 1960, when computers were still gigantic and filled entire rooms.

"Andrew Duncan and Paul Sand — two superb mimes, by the way — are on stage establishing this giant computer, and a multitude of buttons and read-outs covered the entire stage," says Del. "Barbara Harris and Severn Darden enter. Barbara says, 'Ooooh, is that the new computer?' Severn replies, 'No, that's the old computer.' He reaches into his pocket and produces a computer the size of a matchbox. 'Here's the new one!' Duncan and Sand were purple with rage, despite Severn's accurate projection of future computer shrinkage!"

Another candidate for "Worst Crime in Improv" is physical violence on stage that actually results in an actor getting hurt. This is very rare, but occasionally someone who considers himself a "serious actor," whose only previous exposure to improvisation has been a method acting class, lets his honest emotions lead them into violence, usually in the form of a slap, a punch, or a bent finger. This is inconsiderate and self-indulgent, but worst of all, it cools off the audience.

So what happens when a scene requires violence?

Easy. We do it in slow motion.

As Del explains, this accomplishes a lot of things at once, including safety! Fight scenes on stage or in film are impeccably choreographed and rehearsed, and people still get hurt — they are *never* improvised.

Slowing down the action lets the audience see and relish the detail of someone getting punched in the stomach or the face; the face slowly distorts under the fist, and the stomach slowly becomes concave as the eyes pop *slowly*.

It also gives the performers a chance to show off their physical skills. A fight becomes a dance. Shelley Berman was reputed to be so skilled at this, that when he was punched, he could hit the floor and actually *bounce* in slow motion (and this was before Sam Peckinpah made his discovery of *slo-mo* mayhem)!

No matter how careful they are, improvisers constantly sustain a series of small injuries — "furniture bites" — particularly in revue companies with plenty of on-and-off traffic in the dark during blackouts between the scenes. Each company develops its own set of collision reduction guidelines.

"Basically, the best rule is to have the people leaving the stage and the people coming on the stage *use different doors*," says Del, though this is not usually a major concern during a Harold.

"At the Committee in San Francisco, the permanent set

consisted of five doors and two hanging curtains. The safety chant went 'On through the curtains, off through the doors!' This minimized collisions, but did not eliminate them. But, as Keith Johnstone points out, performers are in a state of trance anyway, and tend to not notice the bruises and nicks when they happen.

"I remember coming home after a performance, getting undressed for bed, and having my girlfriend say, 'My God! What happened to your legs?' Purple marks and bleeding shins. Furniture bruises. It's amazing how many different places on stage three bentwood chairs can get!"

Fortunately, as improvisers, we seldom have more to worry about on stage than the chairs and our fellow players, though that wasn't the case when Del was directing the Committee in San Francisco in the late 1960s.

"I decided to do a gag with the stage left door, which was normally hinged at the left and opened *on* stage. I had the door rehinged on the bottom for the Mummy's entrance in 'The Curse of the Tomb — Aieeee!' In this kind of minimalist theatre, a door that opens in a surprising way qualifies as a 'special effect!' On cue, Larry Hankin as the Mummy would unlatch the two bolts and drop the door, entering not so much *through* it, but *on* it," says Del.

"Of course, the inevitable happened. One night during the improv set, a former company member, back for a guest appearance, noticed the new bolts on the back of the door and said, 'What's this?' She unlocked the bolts, and dropped the door on the head of Jessica Meyerson, the producer's wife!"

THE QUESTION GAME

This is a game for more experienced players — unless an actor is capable of improvising a decent scene without a handicap, he shouldn't try it in public. Any time a performer does a scene under a handicap, it requires plenty of concentration, whether they are improvising a scene in verse, in different literary or cinematic styles, or performing when the first and last lines of dialog have already been selected (all of which are valuable games, as well).

In the Question Game, the idea of question-asking is fully embraced. During this exercise, only questions are allowed! A scene is built with no declarative statements at all. This can be surprisingly difficult. Only true questions are allowed, not statements bent into interrogatives by adding "don't you?" or "isn't it?" at the end. And to increase the pressure, the audience is encouraged to boo mistakes!

KEY POINTS FOR CHAPTER TEN
*Find your function or role in every game.

CHAPTER ELEVEN
How to Do a Harold

A Harold utilizes anything and everything included in this book. Harolds can be made up of a limitless number of formats, although most of them are based on the structure described in this chapter.

Harolds are composed of three basic elements: scenes (involving two to four players), games (usually involving the full company) and one-person monologs.

Teams begin by asking for a suggestion from the audience. They then personalize the suggestion and develop an attitude, which is expressed through the opening game (which can take many different forms).

After the opening, the players begin the first round by improvising scenes (three seems to be the standard number). These are followed by a game, and then the scenes return for further development. Another game follows, and the scenes are brought back for a third time, though not all scenes will return. The Harold can end with any one of the scenes, or with another game.

That's Harold in a nutshell — the details are a little more extensive.

TAKING SUGGESTIONS FOR A HAROLD

When players ask an audience for a theme, it's best to ask for a simple, mundane subject, so the actors can elevate it into something vastly profound. It's always exciting to watch a team take a topic as trivial as "wet cardboard" and discover the meaning of life while exploring it. The subject can be a simple object, an issue, or even a question, such as "Why do we fight?" Of course, if the players take a question, they should not try to answer it in the opening. They aren't concerned with answering questions, only exploring the possibilities.

Players should try to take the first suggestion given by the audience, for two reasons. If the players hesitate, the audience members will probably shout out dozens of suggestions, drowning each other out and making it hard to choose. More importantly, if the players hesitate very long, the audience will think they aren't capable of improvising about any given topic (which of course they are). Sometimes a drunken audience member will shout out "hemorrhoids" or some equally inspired thought. A player is certainly within his rights to explain to the audience that while they are perfectly capable of doing such a Harold, do they really want to watch hemorrhoids on stage for the next half hour? A more appropriate suggestion usually follows.

It is also important to remember that the Harold is *not about* the theme. It is only *inspired* by the theme. The Harold is about the ideas extracted from the theme by each individual player, starting with the opening exercise. These ideas are used for the scenes and games that the team is about to improvise.

When the players receive their suggestion and begin to extrapolate their ideas, they should always avoid making obvious statements. Instead, they should raise the suggestion to a higher level. For example, if the theme was "color," it would be a waste of time to name every color in the spectrum during the opening exercise. It's important to get as many different ideas as there are players, so that the theme is incorporated on plenty of levels.

The theme of "color" could inspire ideas about art, racism, exploitation in journalism, sports commentating, and a host of others. When this is added to personal experiences and memories triggered in the players' minds, the list is unlimited. A theme like "color" can even inspire ideas for emotional states ("green with envy," "purple with rage"). All of the possibilities can be used on different levels in the work. And, all possible ideas are shared in the opening, which occurs immediately after the suggestion is taken.

PERSONALIZING THE SUGGESTION

Everyone has a personal experience or feeling that can be related to any suggestion, so there is no reason for a player's mind to go blank when the group is given a suggestion.

When the Baron's Barracudas were performing one night, they were given "futon" for a suggestion. However, Howard did not know what a futon was. Therefore, his opening monolog started off with this confession: he went on to say that the word reminded him of some sub-atomic particle, and went on speculating until his teammates politely explained that a futon was a type of folding couch or mattress, and the group continued onward. In this case, Howard didn't even have to know what the suggestion meant in order to personalize the subject. On those rare occasions when a player doesn't know what a suggestion means, all he has to do is ask his teammates on stage!

Personalizing a suggestion — drawing on past experiences or feelings — brings ideas to the player's mind.

In a recent workshop, the topic suggested for the Harold was "pets." During the opening, which in this case was a series of monologs, one of the students became stuck and stopped the game. He felt he could not play the game because he had absolutely *nothing* to say about pets. Charna asked him if he owned a pet; he replied that he did not, and would never want one (certainly an impulse strong enough to inspire a monolog!). He said that pets were as big a responsibility as having a child. "Who wants that responsibility?" he asked.

He clearly had a personal feeling on the subject, and as soon as he realized it, the rest was all downhill. His idea of comparing pets to raising children became stronger, and began to include ideas from other monologs, as well. When a teammate mentioned that she had just had her 16-year-old dog put to sleep, he ended the monolog game with, "Try doing *that* to a kid!"

THE OPENING

The opening is the most important part of the Harold, since it is the foundation of the entire piece. You can't build a house starting from the roof down, and an improviser has to use the elements introduced in the opening to build scenes and games.

Every bit of information shared by the players in the opening will be remembered and used. Harold is very economical — nothing is lost.

Because the laughs in a Harold come from the connections made in the work, the audience has to see where the information originated. In other words, they are involved with the development of the piece right from the very start. The audience feels they are "in" on the jokes, since they have witnessed their creation, and they are (hopefully) encouraged to laugh even more.

For the actors, the opening is the information sharing process. It is where the players discover each other's points of view on the theme, and the place where the group mind must begin to develop. The attitudes and emotions displayed in the opening give helpful hints on relationships among the group members — information that will provide inspiration for the future scenes.

This information sharing process can begin in many ways. The theme itself may inspire the team to create an original, never-before-done opening. Most of the time, however, a Harold will begin with commonly used openings like monologs, pattern games, songs, or combinations of the above. The Pattern Game is discussed in an early chapter, but monologs are just as useful in a Harold.

MONOLOGS

A monolog in a Harold is an opportunity to remember and then share a past experience. Players must *remember*, not *invent*. This book was titled *Truth in Comedy* because there is nothing funnier than the truth, so players must keep their monologs honest. Audiences relate to someone who is telling the truth, and usually know when a performer is inventing.

When a theme is given, each player tells a personal story that is inspired by that theme. It is important for the monolog ideas to be different from each other, so the team has more ideas to draw from. The more chaos existing in the pot of information, the easier it is to tie things together. *Out of chaos comes order* is a law of physics that also applies to improv.

If the group only discussed one idea, then there is nothing to pull together. If the theme was "dog," it would not be a good idea for everyone to talk about how much they miss their dogs.

Monologs should also be kept short, certainly less than a minute. When monologs are used in between a Pattern Game for a little variation during the opening, there should be no more than three of them, or the opening will take much too long. Lengthy openings cause the game to lose energy, and usually provide too much information for the players *and* the audience.

A series of monologs doesn't have to be limited to the opening in a Harold, however. Three back-to-back monologs can be used between scenes — in place of a group game — in most Harolds. A player may even "freeze" a scene (usually by such unsubtle means as saying "Freeze!" and stepping forward) to deliver a monolog inspired by that very scene. When he is finished, he "unfreezes" the scene, which is hopefully affected by the monolog as it resumes.

One example of this type of monolog was done by Ian Gomez. Two players were portraying high school students challenging each other to a fight. The scene slowed down when the two of them didn't want to enact a fight on stage (even in slow motion), and so Ian froze the scene and said, "In high school, some people were afraid of me because I'm half Puerto Rican, but there were others who weren't threatened by me at all, because I'm also half Jewish."

When he finished, the scene continued where it left off. Randy Hassan said in a tough Puerto Rican accent, "I'd punch your lights out, but I have to get dressed for Seder."

Ian's monolog helped the scene to find a direction, and Randy astutely picked up the gift and made it work.

There are different variations to the monolog as an opening game, each used for different reasons. One of these games, called the Rant, is terrific for building energy.

THE RANT

A Rant contains elements similar to the Cocktail Party and Conducted Story. It is built through individual monologs that eventually connect, but is performed without a conductor (although one of the players may serve as a conductor when the group is first learning the game).

Rants consist of the actors delivering loud, angry monologs on a particular aspect of the theme. Each player breaks his monolog up into "beats," which then intercut with the monologs of the other players. The basic information in each monolog is given within the first two beats. After that, the players begin speaking more quickly and angrily, and speeches begin to overlap. After the second beat, players seldom speak more than one or two lines, instead using it as an opportunity to make connections with the ideas from other monologs.

Experienced improvisers know how to execute a flashy and impressive ending to the opening Rant. In unison, the players raise the decibel level of their speeches, giving the appearance that they are all ranting and raving madly for a brief moment — which they are! Suddenly, simultaneously, they cease talking. Then, one player sums up the group Rant with one quick line that pulls together as many trains of thought as possible.

The Rant provides an interesting spin to the traditional opening monologs; it also sends the players off on a high wave of energy, so they begin their Harold fully charged, with adrenaline pumping.

Chris Farley says the first time he ever performed the Harold before an audience with the ImprovOlympic, his team opened with a Rant. He likened it to his experiences playing football. "I remember Charna was reluctant to put me on stage because she had never seen me work before," recalls Farley. "We did a Rant to open, which is kind of unusual — teams usually start with a Pattern Game. I tried to explode and get the first hit, like I used to do in football, so the butterflies are gone and I can play the game. When I exploded off the Rant, the butterflies *were* gone. I guess I did a pretty good job, because Charna kept letting me go up on stage!"

One variation on the Rant is called Conducted Gripes, or, as it was originally called, the Symphony of Social Criticism.

"Our company invented that game," recalls Tim Kazurinski. "We'd take a pet peeve or a social injustice. Bruce Jarchow always conducted them so well — he'd have two people going, then a different two people, there would be solos, *fortissimo* and *sotto voce* — he did it wonderfully.

"Bruce was always looking for somebody with an 'out,' and if nobody had one, he'd give it to me. I always had to start working on one in advance, because I knew that son of a bitch was going to stick it to me again," he laughs.

ROUND ONE (1A, 1B, 1C)

After the opening game, the players should have an idea of how their theme might affect the upcoming scenes. With this information in the back of their minds, they are ready to begin the first round of scenes.

Experienced players know that since each of the scenes returns, they don't need to complete them during the first round (in fact, if a scene is completed, there's really no need for it to come back at all!).

The scenes in a Harold are usually (but not always) done in three beats, based on a game called the Time Dash. A Time Dash is a three-part scene, with an unlimited passage of time between each of the three beats.

Players *establish* a relationship in the first beat. Since relationships are always in the process of changing and mutating, after the actors have discovered their relationship in the first beat, it changes to its *potential* in the second, and comes to a *resolution* in the third.

Since there are no limits to the imaginary time spans in between the beats, the players don't have to live out every agonizing moment of their relationship — only enough of it to understand the changes.

The first round of the Harold usually involves three scenes, consisting of the first beats of three separate Time Dashes (scenes 1A, 1B, and 1C). A large group may occasionally involve four or even five scenes in the first beat (1D and 1E), but only the strongest three scenes are usually brought back for the second and third beats. In fact, the third beat may only contain one scene; if it's a strong one, it ties together the threads running through the Harold, or otherwise proves to be a good closer for the piece.

Whether there are three, four, or five opening scenes, it's important that they all stay far apart from each other in the beginning; that way, it's even more impressive when they finally come together. The scenes may even connect physically by the end of the piece, though this only happens if they are very far apart at the beginning. Just like a tripod or a teepee, if the legs are too close together, it topples over!

After the relationships are established in the first beats of the three scenes, it's usually time for a game. Taking place between each round of scenes, games are used to heighten the theme on levels that may not have been dealt with in the individual scenes.

Most games involve the entire company. Even if a player doesn't begin the game, he is naturally expected to support it.

"I was never much good at initiating games — I was too dumb for that," jokes Chris Farley. "Once somebody initiated it, I loved to jump right in, but I wasn't real good at the games."

Many games are invented on the spot, with the inspiration coming from the theme. Other games are learned in workshops. Just about every group exercise described in this book could serve as a game within a Harold, but again, there are no rules. The players might even deliver three monologs, instead of a game.

ROUND TWO (2A, 2B, 2C)

The relationships have been established in the first round of scenes, so the players further them in the second. The scenes may pick up exactly where they left off, or they might have advanced 50 years into the future. There are no restrictions!

Without forcing the connections, the players may notice their scenes affecting other scenes in minor ways. They may occur at the same location, or they may be encountering similar problems. Again, there are no limits to the ways the scenes connect.

After the second beats of the three scenes are completed, it is time for a second game. Just as the scenes may affect the game, the information generated in the games may also end up affecting scenes. Everything can connect.

ROUND THREE (3A, 3B, 3C)

This is the final beat, although all three scenes may not return. Some may have completed themselves more quickly than others, so if they seem to have achieved a logical ending, there is no need for them to go on.

Things are tied up in the final scenes. The third beat is usually the shortest of the three, as well. This is not the time to bring in new information or start a new adventure, but to wrap up the existing matters.

Here the scenes must resolve individually, and reflect each other's ideas to the fullest. On a good day, there will be major connections among the scenes at this point in the Harold, and a group statement will emerge; the scenes may even tie together naturally. *But*... if the players try to force scenes that really don't belong together, it can be as jarring as fingernails across a blackboard.

It isn't always necessary to physically connect the scenes. It can be just as enjoyable to see them reflect ideas or opinions derived from the group mind.

A SAMPLE HAROLD

Describing the structure of a Harold is important, but seeing how an actual Harold develops may be even more helpful. This is a synopsis of the Harold that grew out of the Pattern Game described early in this book, based on the theme of camera.

Opening Pattern Game: "Camera"

"High school... high speed... dope... Indy 500... Most likely to... crash and burn... In Memoriam... Viet Nam... Don't write on the wall... smokin'... I caught you... Smile!... I think I got it... Clap... I think I got it... The answer is... Let's see what develops... I think I got it... photo-finish... by a nose... buy a vowel... by the hair of my chinny-chin-chin... buy a bond... propaganda... buy it... Viet Nam... bye bye... dope... speed... it happened so fast... Indy 500... high speed... high school."

Round One:

1A — Two high school boys smoke dope in the restroom, while searching for their names in the graffiti on the walls. Finding their names, they proudly read their sexual exploits, as well as those of others. One girl in particular seems to be prominently mentioned in every message. They find a line reading, "Sue has V.D.," and look frightened.

1B — A married couple packs their belongings in preparation for their move. They are leaving the country. The man finds his old high school yearbook. He looks up his picture and proudly reads his stats: track star, All-American, voted most likely to succeed. He seems guilty about moving.

1C — News commentators report events of the day, including car wrecks, racing results, and photo coverage of casualties in Viet Nam.

First Group Game:

The team improvised a game which they called "A Picture Is Worth a Thousand Words." The actors performed their own "slide show," freezing in position to depict historical events which reveal ironic truths about political and social issues.

Round Two:

2A — The same boys from the high school scene are now in a foxhole. They aren't as cocky as they were before, and one of them abuses cocaine to overcome the pain from a wound.

2B — The man tells his wife that the president has declared amnesty for draft dodgers, and they decide to return to the U.S.

2C — A newscast still shows reports from the Viet Nam era, while making connections to the other scenes and the game.

Second Group Game:

The team presented a narration game, where they were presenting an inside view of the workings of the C.I.A. The game dealt with surveillance techniques and conspiracy theories, ranging from Watergate to the assassination of JFK (connections to the theme included information on the C.I.A. doctoring photos of Lee Harvey Oswald).

Round Three:

3A — One of the two boys sits in front of the Viet Nam Memorial in a wheelchair, searching for the name of his buddy on the wall, and then proudly reads it out loud.

3B — The couple is photographing their new baby. She notices a man on TV who seems to look like one of the guys they went to high school with (the boy from the first scene).

3C — The newscasters are now showing the Viet Nam Memorial. This becomes a three-way split scene; the video of the wall has the guy from 3A looking for his buddy's name. The couple is watching this on TV — the husband is not surprised that his wife, *Sue*, recognizes the guy. She knew *all* of the guys in that school!

The lights fade after the boy sits in silence at the Memorial, and the newscaster closes with a final remark: "That's the news. Tune in at ten for an interview with the winner of the Indy 500."

ENDINGS

Scenes do not have to end in the same order that they began. In the third round, an organic ending usually appears. Perhaps one of the scenes emerges for a fourth time, or all of the players find a natural way to be in the final scene. A third group game or an improvised song may evolve out of the last scene. The players may even break out of the last scene and do monologs that sum up the proceedings and connect back to the opening monologs. As seen in the above example, the three scenes may all physically connect.

Music is always a good way to end a Harold, and is usually an audience-pleaser, whether the song evolves organically within the final scene, or there is a call for a madrigal or other group number.

"I loved the madrigals, and I loved singing," says Chris Farley. "It makes a Harold a lot of fun. My group sang quite a bit — maybe too much, using it in scenes and such! A lot of our Harolds ended in some sort of song. Singing was always a vital part of our Harolds."

Of course, there is no one way to end a Harold. The players can only follow the moment, and do what the piece requires.

The only way is the organic way. An ending cannot be decided until the spur of the moment — that's improvisation!

LEVEL OF THE WORK

There were many interesting levels working in the preceding Harold.

Events in the newscasts kept showing the time spans of the other scenes in each round. The reports displayed the changing of American ideals, particularly on the subject of patriotism. This is particularly reflected in the husband-wife scene, when the man is looking at his old yearbook. He proudly reads about himself as an "All-American," as he packs to flee the country. Throughout the reports, there were also connections to the scenes that are too numerous to mention.

The first physical connection of the actual scenes comes when the woman sees and remembers the vet on TV, which was occurring in the split-scene format. But there was another level to this connection. The innocent high school boys reading the bathroom wall to discover how many classmates had screwed the same woman, is reflected in the scene of the vet reading the names on the Viet Nam Memorial. The woman becomes the symbol for America when it becomes apparent that the vet is still reading on a wall the names of men who have been "screwed."

It's interesting to see the different levels of ideas extracted from one theme, through a group mind. In another Harold, the theme of "money" inspired various levels of fraud, scheming, plagiarism, and impersonation.

One scene depicted Exxon executives lying to the public about their efforts to clean up the Alaskan oil spill.

A second scene featured underwater characters, including two fish, and Bruce the Shark — the King of the Sea. In the first beat of this scene, the fish were able to pull a scam on Bruce because they were pink, and could easily blend in with the coral whenever Bruce was on the prowl (obviously, this took place before the Exxon spill). In the second beat, the fish were distressed because the coral was stained black, and they could no longer blend in.

The third scene involved two aspiring rock stars who deliberately plagiarized the songs of famous musicians to reap the publicity. They become so famous as plagiarists that, in a later beat, a fan asks one of them for an autograph, but requests that he sign it "James Brown." In the final beat, one of the singers becomes an Elvis impersonator.

Clearly to this group, money represented fraud and power, with its images of the "king" (Bruce the Shark and Elvis), and the powerful Exxon.

LIFE IS A SLOW HAROLD

The Harold is an incredible tool for teaching improvisation, but it teaches other lessons, as well.

Strangely enough, many of the Laws of Physics and the Laws of Improvisation are similar (including such principles as order out of chaos, anything can happen, the cycles and patterns that naturally occur). Understanding these laws makes life a bit easier to understand. We learn lessons from the patterns in our lives, and start to believe that there are no coincidences.

A few years ago, one ImprovOlympic group was hired to write a show. Since everyone had so many ideas they wanted to work on, the members wrote up their ideas separately, and then came together a week later to read them. The scenes not only connected, but had direct references to each other — yet they were written completely separate!

Needless to say, the group was in shock. They could understand how something like this could happen while on stage improvising together, when they were listening to and using each other's ideas to make connections. But how could they make connections while physically separated?

Improvisers have been trained to notice the connections

in everything, which may be the answer. The connections are always there; they run through our work and through our lives.

When you notice the richness of connections in a Harold on stage, then you can go out and live your own Harold.

You will, too, you know. You can't help it!

KEY POINTS FOR CHAPTER ELEVEN

*The suggestion is the inspiration to discover the theme.

CHAPTER TWELVE
Harold As a Team Sport

The ImprovOlymic: Why a Sport?
How to Direct a Harold Competition

A performance situation is obviously very different from an improv workshop, so the director's responsibilities in those two situations are also going to be very different.

In a workshop, the director prepares (and sometimes trains) the group in preparation for a performance.

But after the director has trained and inspired the actors, once the show is set and the actors hit the stage, the director's job is done. When the actors step on stage, their performance is out of the hands of their director (*after* the show is over, of course, the director gives notes to the performers).

A director often employs a technique in workshop situations to keep players on track while they are improvising informally.

While a scene is going on, the director makes an off-stage suggestion. The actors continue their scene, incorporating the director's suggestion without breaking their reality.

Such active directing is used if a scene can be put back on track with a quick comment. Sometimes, a scene can actually be frozen to point out a missed game move: the action is then resumed, allowing the players to successfully complete the scene. But most of the time we choose not to interrupt the scene, because the mistakes often lead to more interesting discoveries. Afterward, the scene is critiqued and the problem is discussed.

Again, all of these techniques are fine for the classroom, but it's important to remember that the classroom is where they should stay!

Some directors insist on coaching players from the "sidelines" during their performance. Bad idea! This works against any possibility of discovery on stage. It takes away the responsibility of the players to support and justify each other's mistakes, which is how the discoveries come about. Most importantly, it makes the horrendous assumption that the ideas of the director are more important than the ideas discovered through the group mind.

Del's motto in putting up an improv show has always been "light fuse and run!"

This book is designed to provide the reader with new ideas on comedy, and to furnish enough information for creating a Harold team. Anyone who follows the suggestions may not have the benefit of Charna and Del's coaching in person, but then, Harolds created strictly within the guidelines in these pages may lead to more interesting discoveries!

This is really a guide book, to guide readers to making their own discoveries. After all, in improv, the only rule is that there are no rules.

Writing this book is the authors' equivalent of lighting the fuse and running. The explosion is up to you.

About the Authors

Charna Halpern

The only living creator of long-form improvisation, Charna Halpern is the director of the i.O. Theatre in Chicago (formerly ImprovOlympic) and i.O. West in Los Angeles. Her theatres have been the conduit of talented performers and writers on television shows *such as* Saturday Night Live, The Daily Show, The Colbert Report, Late Night with Conan O'Brien, *and* Mad TV, *as well as film. Under Halpern's guidance, the i.O. Theatres are producing the next generation of artistic geniuses.*

In addition to Truth in Comedy, *Charna is the author of a new book and DVD,* Art by Committee, *a guide to advanced improvisation.*

The late **Del Close***'s life was virtually a history of American improvisation.*

Mr. Close started his comedy career with Mike Nichols and Elaine May in the Compass Players *in St. Louis during the 1950s. Moving on to Second City and eventually to San Francisco as creator and director of the legendary radical political satire comedy troupe* The Committee, *Del returned to* Second City *in 1973 and remained for twelve years as its highly successful director. He was co-creator of* SCTV *with Andrew Alexander as well as "House Metaphysician" for three seasons of* Saturday Night Live. *He is credited for honing the talents of John Belushi, Bill Murray, Gilda Radner, Betty Thomas, John Candy, and many others.*

Close's dream of creating an art movement came to fruition when he hooked up with his partner Charna Halpern where they created long-form improvisation at the ImprovOlympic. Together they changed the face of improvisational comedy.

A life-long devotee of improvisational comedy, Del Close died in Chicago on March 4, 1999 at the age of 64.

Writer, performer, and improviser **Kim "Howard" Johnson** *is proud to be a member of the Baron's Barracudas, the first house team of the ImprovOlympic, where he studied and collaborated with Del Close and Charna Halpern. Howard is the author of four books on the Monty Python team, including the bestselling* The First 280 Years of Monty Python, *and is the co-writer (with John Cleese) of the DC Comics graphic novel* Superman: True Brit. *He has served John Cleese as personal assistant, writer and researcher, lackey, and whipping boy. He has also worked as an award-winning writer and editor for newspapers and magazines, and is a screenwriter whose collaborators include Terry Jones and Jonathan Winters. He is a failed men's clothing salesman, chicken fryer, and corporate toady.*

He lives with his wife Laurie Bradach and son Morgan. He is currently writing a film script based on the life of Del Close.

Order Form

Meriwether Publishing Ltd.
PO Box 7710
Colorado Springs CO 80933-7710
Phone: 800-937-5297 Fax: 719-594-9916
Website: www.meriwether.com

Please send me the following books:

_____ **Truth in Comedy #BK-B164** $17.95
by Charna Halpern, Del Close and Kim "Howard" Johnson
The manual of improvisation

_____ **Art by Committee #BK-B284** $22.95
by Charna Halpern
A guide to advanced improvisation (book & DVD)

_____ **112 Acting Games #BK-B277** $17.95
edited by Gavin Levy
A comprehensive workbook of theatre games

_____ **Acting Games #BK-B168** $16.95
by Marsh Cassady
A textbook of theatre games and improvisations

_____ **Improvisation for Actors and Writers** $17.95
#BK-B269
by Bill Lynn
A guidebook for improv lessons in comedy

_____ **The Ultimate Improv Book #BK-B248** $17.95
by Edward J. Nevraumont, Nicholas P. Hanson and Kurt Smeaton
A complete guide to comedy improvisation

_____ **Group Improvisation #BK-B259** $15.95
by Peter Gwinn with additional material by Charna Halpern
The manual of ensemble improv games

These and other fine Meriwether Publishing books are available at your local bookstore or direct from the publisher. Prices subject to change without notice. Check our website or call for current prices.

Name: _____ e-mail: _____

Organization name: _____

Address: _____

City: _____ State: _____

Zip: _____ Phone: _____

❏ Check enclosed
❏ Visa / MasterCard / Discover # _____
                                                                          Expiration
Signature: _____ date: _____
                  (required for credit card orders)

Colorado residents: Please add 3% sales tax.
Shipping: Include $3.95 for the first book and 75¢ for each additional book ordered.

❏ *Please send me a copy of your complete catalog of books and plays.*

Now that you've read about the techniques of long-form improvisation in *Truth in Comedy* author Charna Halpern has written a sequel guide to advanced improvisation …

Art by Committee
A guide to advanced improvisation
by Charna Halpern
foreword by Adam McKay

This sequel to the best-selling improv book *Truth in Comedy* is designed to help improv performers move up to the more advanced levels of improvisation. Accompanying the book is a DVD featuring performers in action demonstrating the instructions and ideas covered in the book. The DVD includes performances by four popular improv groups: *Upright Citizens Brigade, Beer Shark Mice, Armando Diaz Theatrical Experience, The Reckoning* and *assorted short clips with Peter Hulne.* Also on the DVD are interviews with many celebrity improv artists including: Tina Fey, Rachel Dratch, Amy Poehler, Stephnie Weir, Tim Meadows, Andy Dick and Adam McKay. *This book of 19 chapters is divided into three parts:* **1. i.O. Art by Committee Forms** *deals with the New Harold, Tag Outs and Monologs.* **2. The Improviser** *is a general commentary of what makes good improvisation.* **3. History** *tells more about Del Close and his work with the author over the years.*

Paperback (144 pages) with DVD
ISBN-13: 978-1-56608-112-2
ISBN-10: 1-56608-112-2

This book/DVD set is available at your local bookstore or from Meriwether Publishing Ltd. at: **www.meriwether.com**